LIVE
FOR
THE
MOMENT

LIVE
FOR
THE
MOMENT

DISCOVERING YOURSELF TO LIVE
EVERY DAY TO THE FULLEST

CRAIG GORDON

BEAVER'S
POND
PRESS

ISBN 13: 978-1-59298-382-7

Library of Congress Catalog Number: 2011920704

Printed in the United States of America

First Printing: 2015

19 18 17 16 15   5 4 3 2 1

Cover and interior design by James Monroe Design, LLC.

Beaver's Pond Press, Inc.
7108 Ohms Lane
Edina, MN 55439–2129
(952) 829-8818
BeaversPondPress.com

I would like to dedicate this book to all those who have overcome obstacles in their lives to find peace and happiness. Without you sharing your experiences in the darkest moments, this workbook would not have been possible.

*I encourage you to continue sharing your life stories by contacting me at **763-571-8285**. Your faith in yourself to have a better day and in myself to steer you down the right path have led you to see a better side of life.*

I would like to thank my parents. They have been loving and inspiring. They have always been supportive in my mission to instill happiness and fulfillment in others.

CONTENTS

INTRODUCTION

The following workbook has been designed in a step-by-step format for those seeking a change in their lives. You will be amazed at what you can do if you have a thirst for a fuller life of happiness, peace, and comfort.

My whole life has been motivated by different things and events. For every negative event, there is always something positive we can take out of it. We can learn how to look at these situations and focus on how this outcome can enable us to become better or happier people. I have been motivated to increase my life satisfaction and climb higher mountains. I have also been inspired by others who have shared their experiences to develop a positive program that you can use to increase your life's longevity.

I have been a business owner of two businesses for more than fifteen years. I previously was a firefighter and emergency medical technician for more than twenty years. I have been a Christian counselor for more than fifteen years at my church. I also do counseling and coaching at my office. I have chaired numerous committees over the years with different organizations. I have run for various political offices in the past: mayor, state representative, and state senator. I was a commissioner on the Fridley Charter Commission for twelve years and an active member of the Fridley Lions Club for fifteen years. I started and sold both a roller derby league and a singles dating service. I have owned a video arcade business.

I attended North Hennepin Community College and graduated with two degrees: associate of arts and associate of applied science. I have attended Metropolitan State University and graduated with a bachelor of arts degree in psychology. I reside in Fridley, Minnesota.

My focus now is to help inspire you to pursue your dream with a strategy and plan. I will continue to add to my work study here and devise additional strategies for obtaining your full potential.

I would encourage you to contact me at **763-571-8285** or **www.liveforthemoment.life** with your success story after completing this workbook. You can also contact me if you want to inquire about a seminar at your location. You may also contact me if you have interest in having me appear as a motivational speaker.

ONE

STEPS TO DISCOVERING YOURSELF

It is so wonderful and awesome to know you are in the right frame of mind. Your life is here and now ready to be energized by your own mindfulness. Are you feeling the power within yourself to feel and experience the moment at hand? It is possible to live in the moment, not tomorrow or in a few hours but right now this very second. Well, keep reading on and discover the ways to increase the power within yourself. Discovering yourself is a process that enables you to realize the power and control you have. When you start to see the potential and capability within you, you realize there is more you can accomplish.

KNOW WHO YOU ARE

It is important to capture the dreams and goals that motivate you. By doing some self-reflection, you can define yourself. By defining yourself, you then see where your strengths and weaknesses are. Oftentimes, we travel through life not knowing who we really are.

How often have you realized that others are defining who you are? Do you feel you are a compassionate person, or is it something you hear from others but are not a believer of? Do you feel you are motivated, or do you believe it only because you hear it from others? These are questions that need some tough answers.

After thinking about it, you realize you believe what others have said about you but you question it sometimes. How can others think you are compassionate when you don't think you are? Believing in yourself is a powerful tool to possess. It is a vital and critical element that determines your level of success. Your success is based on different things that happen, but knowing your personality, thoughts, and beliefs are definitely beneficial to be conscious of.

Make a list of what you hear about yourself from others, and see which of the items you know are true and which ones you have a harder time believing. Find out where the differences lie, and this then will show you how well you know yourself. Your being is always developing and being nurtured. As you increase your mind to observe and take note of your journey through life, your chances of happiness increase. Your mission should be to realize places where you can increase your potential for positive growth. It is a different mission and can be frustrating at times. This mission is a lifetime journey that can take you places where you have never traveled before.

Defining yourself is a process that continues without an end because over time we change. Unless we are conscious of this and adjust, we find ourselves not moving. Ultimately, we become aware of our changes when others point them out. Insight into our beings provides each of us with opportunities that otherwise wouldn't surface.

The challenge we should always put to ourselves is, "Who am I?" This is a challenge that provides valuable knowledge to our very existence and being. If you lost a sense of who you are, then where is your mark in your journey through life? Are you on track to instill energy and motivation in aspects of your life that need it?

DEFINE YOUR GOALS AND DREAMS

Once you have spent time looking at who you are and what makes you tick, you are ready for the next step. Your goals and dreams are in your head, and you need to extricate them. Everyone has goals and dreams, but most fail to make them happen. It is within your power to realize them. They are there and at times you verbally express them only to have them escape your memory. Goals and dreams are always subject to change due to different variables, but one thing needs to be constant and static: your passion to always have your goals and dreams pursued.

Life is before each of us to accomplish and fulfill our own defined expectations. Dreams are the big pictures. Goals lead the way to measure our progress. Dreams are not realized unless we pass certain goals along the way.

List three dreams you have for your life. Remember, these are long-term events that will include several milestones before the dreams are reached.

1. _____

2. _____

3. _____

Goals should be specific, measurable, achievable, realistic, and time-based. Goals can be attached to rewards, thereby increasing your completion. If you reward yourself, the goals become easier to reach. Increase your rewards by increasing your goals. Isn't it amazing what you can accomplish when you have rewards waiting for you?

List up to five goals for each of the dreams listed above. Remember, these goals may not have rewards, but for those that do you will be able to accomplish them sooner and easier.

Dream 1

1. _____

2. _____

3. _____

4. _____

5. _____

Dream 2

1. _____

2. _____

3. _____

4. _____

5. _____

Dream 3

1. _____

2. _____

3. _____

4. _____

5. _____

Look at your goals and dreams constantly, especially in the morning and before you go to bed. By doing this in the morning, you remain focused. By doing this before you go to bed, you continue your thinking on this as you drift away to sleep.

CONDITION YOUR MIND

Our minds are under our direction and control. We can condition our minds to respond in a directed fashion and think particular thoughts. If we put our minds to it and are observant and conscious of our talk, we can see change.

Self-talk is simply what we are telling ourselves. Our minds are always subject to change, but we need to be the ones to change them. Self-talk is always happening behind the scene in our unconscious mind. It is not always obvious because we do things without putting much thought into them. For instance, you walk to your vehicle, open the door, get in, start it up, and drive off. We know what we are doing but are not totally conscious of it because it is automatic and routine.

Let's say you buy quite a bit of groceries, but many of the items are not the healthiest choice. You are not putting much thought into which is the healthiest choice simply because you desire the item, e.g., donuts. Donuts are not a healthy choice, but they are just so good and delicious that you cannot pass them by.

What if you were informed by your doctor that different choices needed to be made? You now would be conscious of this and tell yourself, *no, I cannot buy that this time.* This is an example of making different choices and being completely aware of what's happening. Your self-talk is now becoming conscious and you are having to make a decision about the subject. Your mind is making a temporary change in your routine, but the change is subject to being permanent. Only you possess the power to decide the outcome.

Conditioning our minds is a lifelong process. Some changes happen quicker than others. We can test ourselves and make small changes, noticing the differences. At times, we unconsciously attempt to condition our minds but don't even realize it.

Let's say you have an exciting event coming up, such as a vacation. You are extremely excited and waiting for the time you leave. That excitement turns into psychic energy that for a brief time you hold. The psychic energy is a form of energy that revolves around a particular event or situation. If you are extremely excited about this vacation for different reasons, you are susceptible to being giddy. You have this extra kick in you where you want to leave now, but know it's not quite time yet. You are telling everyone else about this great vacation, and you have a million reasons for being so excited. Your blood pressure might be higher. Maybe you have experienced this high in the past. This feeling you possess is in the form of psychic energy. Your mind was overloaded with this trip, hence the term "psychic," which then was transformed into energy. You probably didn't realize where this energy came from. Once you are on the vacation, you might have noticed coming down from that high or hyper excitement. Well, the energy brought on by this event can be experienced in other ways with more frequency. This is not an easy task, but you can accomplish this by realizing the power you have with the attitude you maintain. Those mornings before you leave are different from other mornings. You wake up with a ton of energy, and your mind temporarily is loaded with energy. This energy can be a constant flow if you desire this. You can condition your mind to retain this energy and use it to energize your goals.

Oftentimes our burst of temporary energy is through indirect means rather than direct means. Conditioning our minds has to happen through a conscious effort. It needs to be constant, and we need to remind ourselves daily of this. Some believe our minds are already preset, and the difficulties in changing this are too much to overcome. We will never use our minds to the fullest potential. The more positive our thinking is, the more we sustain energy.

The more we fill our mind with faith, hope, happiness, and positive thoughts, the more we reap the rewards of such thinking.

The mind is always a work in progress. You can put in what you want, remember or discard what you want, and dictate your thoughts and behaviors. How many times have you noticed your mind drifting off and it takes you a minute to realize where your mind is? The mind has a tendency to drift off, but if you are focused then you are always aware of what you are thinking. Your mind is always entertaining unwanted thoughts, and you want to fight them off. If these thoughts start to pile up en masse, then you can lose sight of your dreams and goals in life. Do you tend to be a follower or a leader? Do you feel everyone else has the better idea? Do you come to a point where you say, *I give up and leave it to someone else*? Do you find yourself asking someone else, *now what*? Sometimes you think you would be better off being someone else because they always have the answers. Well, your mind is no different from the other person's. The only difference is that they have used their mind with the positive attitude and conditioning. Your thinking can be reversed so that you can experience being a leader. This is why it is so important for you to remain focused and always be aware of your thoughts. Positive thoughts move you into action and lead you to completion of your goals. Other thoughts only prolong what you really want.

MOVE INTO ACTION

It's time to move. It's time to make things happen now, not later. You have been called to accomplish and succeed in your pursuit of dreams. Work on keeping these words in your mind. "I can" and "I will" are motivating and inspiring words. They give you energy and drive to overcome any obstacles. If you believe it will happen, you increase your chances for success. You want to believe in yourself. You want to believe in who you are and what you can do.

How many times have you heard that everything is possible? Well believe it, live it, and see your results. If you just spend a little time every day reviewing your goals, then your mind will become conditioned to that. Your mind doesn't know any better unless your train it. As you continue to train your mind, action then happens consistently.

Moving into action is like climbing a ladder, taking one rung at a time—two rungs if you feel the motivation, energy, and inspiration. You might accidentally miss a rung and take a minute longer to catch up. I like using the ladder metaphor because it is about reaching the top. At the top of the ladder, you have realized your goal or dream. You know by reaching the top you can look down and say you made it. Your hard work and positive attitude made the difference. By continuing to climb the rungs, you know your goal is within reach. Each rung can represent anything you want it to. Your dream will be realized and ready for the next ladder of life. How many times did you fall and get right back up the ladder? You decide the length of your ladder and how many steps you want to take. You can decide the time period to get to the top, taking into account any missteps along the way.

While you are moving forward, continue the positive self-talk. You need this to overcome the failures along the way. Don't be surprised if you find a shortcut to your next goal by experiencing failure. Did you realize the power you possessed with your attitude of *You can do anything*? Success always encompasses some setbacks, but they make your success even sweeter. By getting past the setbacks, your confidence and determination grow even stronger. Look at your plan of success much like a road map from one point to another. You do not know what to expect, but you know obstacles will appear. Your plan of success doesn't contain those obstacles because you are unaware of what they might be. It is in fact a road you have not traveled and is full of surprises and opportunities.

Obstacles and mistakes are to be expected before you reach the top because your road map has not been traveled before. Failures allow for learning and create opportunities. You will learn not to make that same mistake again and look for that opportunity to expand your horizons of knowledge. Moving into action is making sure you don't miss the opportunity to seize the moment and make the most of life. Moving into action contains the following components: knowing where you are in life, what you have accomplished in life, and where you are physically and emotionally, and asking yourself what are your expectations in life. Moving into action is your key to success in life. The success is not happening if you remain idle but bound to happen if you remain focused on moving.

Each person has a unique plan and road map to follow, but action doesn't always represent forward progress. Results of an action might be a step backward, but the lesson to be learned is within the process of this action. The results were unintended, but look at what you found. You must always remember where you will finish and remain focused to your mission and target.

CHALLENGE YOURSELF TO HIT YOUR TARGET

I have listed below some examples to start a person thinking about the future. These exercises will assist you in opening your eyes to what can be. You will start seeing the difference in who you are and where you are planning to go. Moving into action must be a planned process with benchmarks to hit and a timetable.

Your behavior plays a role in the change you want to make. The dreams you have and the goals you seek depend on your behavior and attitude. Your attitude toward your desired outcome plays a role in your behavior. If your attitude is upbeat and you feel enthusiastic, your behavior likewise will come out. Your behavior originates from your attitude or simply what you are thinking, whether it is positive or negative. If you are not happy with your behavior, look further into what you are thinking. All behaviors can be broken into actions. For example, seeking a job involves researching the company, putting out your clothes to wear, answering interview questions, and so forth.

Think of a similar example and break down your behavior.

Behavior: _____

Actions of Behavior: _____

_____

_____

_____

Success will be increased if you break the change down into different parts. What about change? You might be hesitant to change for fear of what's on the other side—maybe failure or rejection. The key here as you move into action is to look at all of the positive results that are related to your goals and dreams. You can see by looking at those positive results that your fears can be dissolved. The more items you have listed increases your desire for that change to happen. For example, let's say you desire to be promoted but you believe a co-worker is better liked. You could list as positive results increased pay, continued promotion, and better hours. If you list enough of these, then you become excited and your fear is gone or nominal. You have seen the benefits in changing versus not changing. Make sure the change is realistic.

Think of a small change you could make that is realistic and achievable in a short period of time. Start small and as time goes on give yourself more of a challenge.

Change: _____

Positive Results Exposed: _____

_____

Moving into action requires structure and focus. You need to identify what will work for you and continuously review that plan. Keep the things that work for you, and build upon them while discarding the things that fail. Repetition will increase your chances of success.

Let's look at getting ready for work in the morning. You need to wake up, eat breakfast, get ready, and leave at a particular time. Now it's your turn to list the activity and put structure to it in a logical sequence of events.

Activity: _____

Sequence: _____

_____

Moving into action requires that you expand your knowledge, and feedback is helpful. Do your homework, and learn as much as you can. Then lay out your plan and seek a mentor—a person who will be honest with you and tell you how well you are doing. You are putting your trust and faith in this person to guide you, which will also increase your motivation to change.

For example, you have a co-worker who you have not talked to since a dispute occurred and you now want to try to make amends. You would devise a plan for communication with this person and have a trusted co-worker give you feedback on your progress. Try to think of a situation where you could use this approach.

Event: _____

Your Plan: _____

_____

_____

_____

Trusted Friend: _____

Moving into action is planning a few small successes that amount to the primary goal being accomplished. Each separate, smaller success gives you increased motivation and confidence to finish the overall job.

Let's say you are planning to pursue a high-level job. Your smaller successes would be passing a physical exam, agility test, written test, and interviews. You would focus on each item separately while in the end achieving the overall goal. Put yourself on a road to success. Now think of something you wish to achieve and separate that into various parts.

Overall Goal: _____

Small Successes: _____

_____

_____

_____

Moving into action is going at a pace that gets the job done. This means not being in a rush to get to the end game. Believe it or not, going slower is better and more effective. Enjoy the journey you are about to embark on. You also are more conscious of the change with a better likelihood that it becomes automatic.

One example would be where you plan a trip and all of the activities. You allow the time for each of these activities to fully enjoy and appreciate them. Now it's your turn to think of an example and actually experience the fullest of that activity. List something that you will carry out, and see the results.

Activity: _____

Planned Agenda: _____

_____

_____

Moving into action also means protecting your newly established behaviors. It is easy to lose your gains by not remembering how you made it to that point. You want to protect those gains so that you do not lose ground. There are different things you can use to your benefit to protect your gains such as memory aids, associating with positive individuals, and being in a favorable environment.

Let's say you want to be in bed by 10:00 pm daily. The things you may choose to stay away from might be friends who stay up late, events that end too late, and consumption of excessive alcohol in a bar. List a behavior you want to change that is conducive to your goals and how you will guard against going back to the old way.

New Behavior: _____

_____

_____

Guards to Protect New Behavior: _____

_____

_____

Discovering yourself is a process that is valuable to experiencing success. Your success is based on what you are truly capable of accomplishing. You want to reach for the stars, but always keep your goals truly within reach and grasp. You want your goals to be challenging but also reachable and attainable. Remember to always tell yourself to continue your dream no matter how tough the journey is. Good luck—you really do have the drive and determination to experience success. The choice is yours to make.

TWO

MY PHILOSOPHY ON LIFE

What is your philosophy on life? Have you thought about it long enough to know? It is important for you to know your style, method, and process of life. My philosophy on life can be different from yours because your life is centered on you.

My philosophy on life should open your thinking on this subject. Your philosophy on life is what makes up your life. You can explore your meaning of life through your discovery and interpretation of your own philosophy.

Life can take on many different routes. Some of them are positive, and some of them, unfortunately, are negative. But we are able to learn from the negative situations. We can take positive things from such outcomes and use them to our advantage to strengthen our weaknesses and character. We are all capable of conditioning our minds so that we think positively. Many lessons we learn from life, and the most valuable ones, are generally from the negative situations. We wish the negative situations would not have happened, but how we look at those situations is what matters. We can look at each situation in both positive and negative views. Life is a continual learning experience if we desire. It is our choice. Do we improve upon who we are as people and increase our happiness? The alternative is not one that we desire but need to be conscious of. Every one of us will make mistakes as we make our journey through life. Each of our lives is different. Due to variables that determine life's course, each life is looked at individually. A person may have tougher life experiences than another, and with a tougher life we may need to work at being positive more diligently. Any one of us can respond to what life puts before us, and we are given the choice of how to manage the outcome.

As you continue conditioning your mind to respond in a favorable manner, you will notice the positive attitude you have on life. Your life is always evolving. You have the freedom to pursue your dreams. You have the capability to fulfill your dreams. You have the resources available to assist in your passion for success. If you put your mind to change, then believe in it.

If you imagine and have faith, everything is possible. You must imagine what the change is and possess the faith in your heart. Remember, we are all equals in our society and started with nothing. You do not know your time on Earth nor do we know what it consists of. If we believe that our lives can be shortened at any moment, shouldn't that motivate all of us? If we do not take life for granted, then we should be able to constantly fulfill our own challenges. Life takes many twists and turns. We can be smiling and feel as though we are the happiest people on Earth at one moment only to have the next moment filled with grief and sadness. We don't know what will happen. We do know that death will await us at some point, hopefully when each of us believes our life has been complete.

What would make your life complete? What is it that would bring happiness and joy to you? What do you know about yourself? Your life is always passing before you with opportunities for you to further complete your life. It is within you to arrive at your target. Everyone has a different idea of what happiness, joy, and fulfillment are. Each of us can be moved by what others do. Individuals who desire to help others, such as visiting the sick, may do just that to help complete their lives. That act of service to the sick and needy can inspire others to do the same. Our society revolves around what we do. Our society is built and founded on good but only remains good as long as the individual members continue to make those positive contributions. Your life should always be looked at in the present, not tomorrow or yesterday but now. Where are you in your own life right now? Life has been given to us to make the best choices we can. Every one of us is unique and special. There is not another individual on Earth like you. That uniqueness sets you apart from everyone else to chart your own course in life. It is your decision to bring quality of life to yourself. You have no limitations set and are free to conquer all challenges that lie in front of you. You are free to let your mind go. You are not bound by rules, policies, or procedures. The sky is the limit, and you can put yourself in a position where you can think and dream with no obstructions or difficulty. Your mind has to be engaged in the future. If you could turn a dream into reality right now, what would that dream be?

What have you thought of previously that would change your life substantially? What changes in your life have you wished for? Your life is dictated on what actions you take. Your mind is ready and waiting to be used to the maximum. Do you realize that we can never use our minds to capacity? It will never happen. That is an indication of how we can make things happen. It is what you choose to remember and how you process the data that determines what memory is left in your mind. The negativity in your mind only decreases your potential for success. The negativity deletes room for the vital life happiness data and overrides your thinking process. At some point, your mind is conditioned to think in a particular fashion. Let's say your working hours were 8:00 AM to 5:00 PM for several years and then your hours changed to 11:00 PM to 7:00 AM. Your body changes and conforms to your new working hours. You do not consciously make this happen, but rather your body determines it necessary. Specifically, your mind completes this transition or reconditioning without any conscious effort on your part. You can become a new being, which in time would feel like second nature. It is not easy to do and takes commitment, but it can be done. Character strengths such as loyalty, kindness, and vitality can be learned. You are where you are on these strengths due to your habitual ways of responding to the world.

You are looking from the outside in rather than looking from the inside to the outside. Let's take being overweight, for example. At a point the individual may be overweight and decide to lose weight. The individual is looking from the inside and saying, "I don't want to be overweight and I am going to change this." Many people lose weight who are committed to the plan. Most people become overweight not consciously realizing what was happening. The individual gained too much weight as a habitual way of responding to the world. The individual didn't think about it because it seemed okay at the time. Change in your life can be transformational and positive because it opens you up to experience new things in life and also act in a different way. Initially you might feel uncomfortable doing something new. Understandably that would be a predictable response because it is something new. New behaviors in turn create new experiences. As you experience these new experiences, time will then implement these transitions to your being. At some point, these transitions become more permanent, thus creating a feeling of being second nature to you.

Bringing joy, optimism, or like qualities to your being is doable. If you want more joy in your life, then you must be more open to experiencing sadness, fear, and anxiety. This works the same for passion. Joy is experienced to a greater level if you experience the opposite. Let's say you want to be more optimistic. Learning to think like an optimist is much less important than acting like one. Actions will create more of a positive result than learning to think. If you act like an optimist, your thinking will follow. You can learn to think like an optimist, but not putting that in a behavioral fashion does very little. If you act like an optimist, your thinking will respond in a like manner. Let's say you want to be more courageous. Do you realize that has nothing to do with how afraid you are? It is simply about your level of intensity about your goals, how strongly you feel.

Most people are afraid to speak in front of a large crowd. Most do not ever get comfortable with public speaking. The anxiety is always there. Some public speakers are introverts. I am always nervous speaking in a large group setting, but I continue. I am now comfortable but still nervous about all of my public speaking events. I can recall running for state representative and debating with the incumbent on television. I was extremely nervous, and no hours of practice could have taken care of that. The incumbent had twenty-plus years of service in the legislature, and it seemed my anxiety was here to stay. I survived the debate, and the feedback from the public was extremely positive. It was reassuring and helped me gain the confidence that I could do it again. I was afraid of the debates scheduled, but that didn't deter me from participating in them. I felt so strongly about my goals for the campaign that the debates were going to go on. As you continue to walk in places where you are less comfortable, it is also exciting and rewarding. If you feel strongly about your goals, then fear will not be a determining factor in your decision.

Optimists suffer less and recover much more quickly. Optimists also generally are healthier, are better liked, and have more fun. Their marriages also tend to be stronger. These qualities stem from habits you can learn. More than any other trait, optimism is simply a matter of putting it into practice. This is not necessarily your continually saying positive things but more so a matter of how you behave. You can take the long route and continue the positive self-talk, and that will lead you to the wanted behavior, but there is a faster route. The better route is to feed yourself and grow within optimistic behavior, always moving toward your goals. This takes constant persistence and commitment to train your mind to notice the good things in life. The good life is out there, ready for the taking, and is the result of your brain functioning at its peak. This peak is created when you experience happiness, satisfaction, and completeness, and your purpose in life has been accomplished. I would encourage you to know when these good things happen. Keep a log and write down all of the positive things that have happened. Keep track of what puts a smile on your face or someone else's. By keeping a log, you will reassure yourself that good things in life are happening. Refer back to these often when you feel a doubt.

Life is about looking to the now and future. Keeping a journal improves your life situation. Most people will write down their deepest secrets, mostly negative ones. This doesn't get you in the frame of mind to be looking ahead but rather you feel gloomy and depressed. Do not write down these types of passages. What you want to write down is the future you want out of a negative situation. Clarify the future you are thinking of and what you need to do. As this develops, you will get a better idea of what you really want and develop a plan or road map to get you there. Taking these small steps forward will lead you on to bigger and better results. One small step at a time creates many more steps at such a level that you will not find yourself going backward.

What is your passion in life? Everybody has a passion, but it may have been put in the back of your mind. You may want to fulfill your passion but feel you lack the ability. You have seen others in life possessing this passion. You can see it by how engaged they are, how involved they are, and how dedicated they are to completing the mission. You can reach this level if you so desire. Your fear is probably stopping you from going forward. You want to separate your fear from the reality of what your body and mind are capable of doing. It requires a plan, discipline, ability, and desire. It is so rewarding when you complete something because you know how difficult it was. If it was easy, you would find it less rewarding and fulfilling. If you absorb yourself in what you do, you will lose yourself in that, and failure is a moot point. When you take time to look at your missteps and lose yourself in your mission, you succumb to failure sometimes. Try to stay away from that.

Do you realize that sometimes the thing that scares you the most can be the most fulfilling and satisfying? This doesn't have to be the most difficult thing to accomplish, but rather something that you don't think you can do. What is your joy? Don't you want to enjoy life and have joy for most of your life? Make yourself a promise:

> I promise to live more fully in the present moment and look for joy in all aspects of my life including failure, disappointment, and sickness. I will be joyous even when I'm not in a joyous mood. I will take pleasure even from sadness and learn from it.

Keep this promise posted where you can constantly see it and remind yourself of your vow. This will act as your renewal in your quest for fulfillment in your life. You are missing half of life if you are simply trying to just get by. What satisfaction in life is there in that? Negative things will always find you, and you let them in, forcing yourself to deal with them. Isn't it time you see the pleasures and positive things before you let the bad things through the door? When something good happens to you, share that moment with people. Try to instill in yourself a vivid picture of the moment and keep it in memory to recall it when you desire. The happiest people will tell others of the happening. Try to instill a photograph in your mind of the event. Your life will be much more joyous if you live your life in a guided fashion and be flexible rather than governed. Sometimes you need to take time off, for instance, rather than continue medical school. Oftentimes a person tends to stay in a comfort zone rather than seek an opportunity. If you want to reach your goals, you may have to get out of the comfort zone. Learning to become more joyous takes time. It does not happen overnight or without a conscious effort. Sometimes when you are trying to avoid failure, your goals and opportunities are sacrificed.

Courage is another term that can take on a life of its own. We usually think of courage in a way that represents physical bravery, in other words, the backbone it takes to stand up to a person involving conflict and tension whether you are on the receiving end or wishing to confront the person. But have you ever thought about the courage that is present in your everyday life? This brings on an individual's own manner of bravery, which is much harder to spot. This may involve stepping up to admit a mistake or speaking out against something. There are many examples of your own bravery in your ordinary life. Have you ever went to your supervisor and said something was amiss, and instead of getting a thank you it was a demotion or a negative report in your personnel file? Those kinds of experiences are stressful and take your energy away to do what is right the next time.

Contrary to what many may think, courage is not driven by fearlessness. It is in fact driven by an individual's sense of duty—a strong belief that the person is doing what is right. Oftentimes people who experience these situations say they were afraid. It is not the fear that lies within you but rather the principles and morals that you hold that forced you to take action. Better understanding of these principles helps you to deal with the situations. Your reaction to a particular situation is dependent upon your core belief and moral values and how strong they are. What experiences have you encountered involving the courage to do what was right? What have you learned from the outcomes of these events? I encourage you to set up experiments for yourself. Attempt a few scenarios of putting yourself out there. Look at how much time you spend experimenting in your life now with different things such as foods, reorganizing your house, or shopping. Yet, we hardly spend any time at all experimenting with the ways we can act as a person. If you add flexibility to this experiment, chances are you will be energized and enjoy the freedom of stepping out of your normal habits. Over the long term, if you continue to find ways to step out, you are only getting closer to the person you want to be. In the short term, you could surprise yourself and see the world in a different light. That alone could be rewarding and a unique kind of internal adventure for yourself.

There is something to be said for magical thinking. Is there something in your life that has a magical perspective to it? Maybe it was an experience of some kind or some inanimate object that you could feel some magic looking at it. I would guess there is some magical thinking going on in your life. This thinking is everywhere. What about Santa Claus? We do not find this on our own but rather passed on. Our parents bring this into our lives, and we believe it until such a time when reality sets in. But until this time arrives, you can probably remember this thinking going on. Other magical thinking we find on our own and incorporate into our being without knowing it and realizing our line of thinking patterns are observed and followed. One pattern is day follows night. We actually desire these patterns because the alternative is surprises, and we lose control. Look at the professional sports athletes who might wear the same piece of clothing or perform the same ritual over and over and continue winning. Who could argue with their success, and yet no one would bet that's the reason for winning.

What about stress and personal events? Is there any magical thinking happening to you? I can recall narrowly being missed by a moving vehicle. The driver was not paying attention to his driving and looked at the last second to avoid this accident. What does this mean, if anything? Events of this nature can move you to magical thinking. Although I am a rational man, events do happen that cannot be explained rationally. There are circumstances where you are led to believe that possibly someone or something is directing your life. In my event, the most direct and first thought was that this driver was trying to kill me. But secondary thoughts crept in containing this magical thinking.

Many layers of magical thinking exist. Most people would freely acknowledge that most of their being doesn't believe but some of their being does belong. Look at the beliefs that you might hold that on the surface you do not acknowledge. For example, you turn your high beams on as you approach a street light. At that moment, that street light goes out. You know that there is no factual basis for this coincidence, but you perceive that casual relation. Our visual systems refuse to believe in these types of coincidences. Magical thinking may not be something you have experienced yet, but the capability of your doing this is present. It is healthy to be a magical thinker just as long as your thinking does not interfere with your everyday functioning.

Previous studies and experiments have concluded that those who lack the ability to enjoy pleasure are unmagical. If you experience a substantially high level of continuous magical thinking, then you are suspected of having a disorder, e.g., obsessive-compulsive disorder. Magical thinking can be in the form of a wish. How many times have you been told to make a wish before you blow out the birthday candles? You probably don't believe that a wish would actually come through from this direct act, but you are led to believe this if even for a moment. Magical thinking can also come in the form of touching an object, such as a plane, and believing that the plane will stay aloft and land with no problems. An act such as this can start by just being in awe of the large airplanes, and through magical thinking the act continues. This brings peace of mind to the flight. This ritual act and similar ones are used most often when there is little cost attached. Other inclusive variables are when the outcome is uncertain or beyond your control and when the consequences of failure are substantial. These people who truly are vested in their trust of these rituals exhibit what is called *illusion of control*. This is the belief that they hold more influence within the world than they really do. I am not saying that this is a bad delusion. This sense of control can motivate people to work harder than they otherwise would. It is within your control to determine to what extent you believe in a ritual.

What about this magical thinking concept? Believing that a just world exists puts our minds at ease and gives us a feeling of contentment. The drawback to pushing this to the extreme, though, is that it can deter you from fighting for more justice. If you truly believe that justice is in the right order and working, then why would you believe additional justice is needed? There is a liability to believing that all things are right in the world and no changes are needed. The choice always remains in your hands as to where your magical thinking is and where you place it in your everyday living.

Every one of us has worth when we enter this world. This worth cannot be taken away no matter how much someone tries. This worth can be described as lovable, equal, valuable, acceptable, and adequate. This is something we have forever. The problems are never somewhere else or with someone else, but rather with you. That is why you want to resolve and deal with your situation rather than change the other person who caused you pain. Never change from who you are, and believe in your worth despite the intense pain you may feel to make the necessary changes.

THREE

SELF-REFLECTION EXERCISES

Self-reflection exercises are beneficial in realizing where you are and where you have been, dealing with it in real time. You may not ever have asked yourself these questions and your answers could set you free. You may have something hiding inside that you are afraid to face, or you may not have realized something is there holding you back. These questions may also spark something else that you need to deal with. Self-reflection on your past is important to knowing you are free. Once you are free, your journey starts with a clean slate. You will not need to worry about the past catching up to you because you have taken care of it.

Your life should consist of self-reflection at times. Life can become routine and non-inspiring if you allow yourself to continue that pattern of behavior and thinking. Jump start your life, and see if anything in the past is keeping you from success now. Do not fear facing something unpleasant or traumatic. It is only you who has the key to enter and set yourself free. Rid yourself of all in your life that is not useful, beautiful, pleasant, or joyful. Also, remember that situations always will change. Your situation in some way will evolve into another event, either progressing to being more positive or negative. Your life may not have been the best of times, but remember the best is yet to come.

As you complete the self-reflection exercises, keep in mind the following:

- The best is yet to come.

- You have the key to unlock the past.

- Set yourself free.

- Forgive and free yourself of anything negative or unpleasant.

- You have the control to change.

- Make today the day you commit to being free.

1. List all of your accomplishments.

_____

_____

_____

2. List all of your strengths.

_____

_____

_____

3. List all of your weaknesses.

_____

_____

_____

4. What do you feel good about, e.g., job, family, finances?

_____

_____

_____

5. What jobs have you had, and what have you learned from each one?

_____

_____

_____

6. List all of the traits you possess, e.g., sincere, generous, loyal?

_____

_____

_____

_____

7. How is your relationship with your family?

Parents: _____

Sister(s): _____

Brother(s): _____

8. Where are your finances sitting?

_____

_____

_____

9. Where are you spiritually?

_____

_____

_____

10. Where would you like to be in

5 years: _____

10 years: _____

20 years: _____

11. What was your upbringing like, e.g., loving, violent?

_____

_____

_____

12. Were you raised in an environment where your parents were

	Mother		**Father**	
	Yes	No	Yes	No
Alcoholic	___	___	___	___
Drug users	___	___	___	___
Abusive	___	___	___	___
Smokers	___	___	___	___

13. What have been some of your dreams?

_____

_____

_____

14. What dreams, if any, have you had that have come true?

_____

_____

_____

15. Are you closest to your mother or father, and what are the differences?

Mother: _____

_____

_____

Father: _____

_____

_____

16. What is your level of education?

_____

_____

_____

17. Have you thought about further education?
Yes___ No___
If you have, but have not pursued it, what has
stopped you?

_____

_____

_____

18. What are some of the things you would have done
differently in the past, e.g., been more caring with
siblings?

_____

_____

_____

19. Describe some personal habits that are important to you.

_____

_____

_____

20. If you had three wishes at your disposal, what would they be?

_____

_____

_____

21. What are the holidays like for you and your family when you get together?

_____

_____

_____

22. When do you feel the most afraid?

_____

_____

_____

23. If you could accomplish only one thing in your life, what would it be?

_____

_____

_____

24. What brings you the most pleasure, and how does it feel when you experience that?

_____

_____

_____

25. Is life looking great for you at the moment? Describe your current emotional state.

_____

_____

_____

26. Who is your closest friend, and what do you like best about that person?

_____

_____

_____

27. Describe your parents' relationship with each other.

_____

_____

_____

28. How do you act when you're angry?

_____

_____

_____

29. What are your thoughts on medications? Do you consider them helpful?

_____

_____

_____

30. When you are feeling down and lonely, who do you turn to for support?

_____

_____

_____

31. Is there anything in the past that you have not let go of and forgiven?

_____

_____

_____

FOUR

FAITH AND PRAYER

Faith is a term that some of us can discuss with conviction. We know what it means to have faith instilled in us. For others, it is something that is not believed in. And others seem to have different points in their lives where they believe that faith has intervened.

Which category do you fall into? Faith is something that is not explainable in certain terms and not visible on the surface in some. Faith is something people hold dearly and is a fundamental truth. It is not a term that is easily definable, yet we live by it every day even if we do not consciously make ourselves aware of it.

How many times have you heard people ask what faith is or where is your faith? Faith is similar to love. "How much do you love a person?" is a question that is frequently asked of each other but is not easily defined. "Do you have faith?" is a question that not everyone can answer without hesitation. The faith issue is one that people think about because it involves interpretation of their meaning of faith.

Do you have faith? What is faith to you? Do you live by faith every day? These are questions that we may have asked ourselves. We may not have fully determined our own meaning and the questions still remain. The faith issue can be a complex one, depending on our interpretations of what it means.

Other questions asked are "Where do you find faith?" and "How can you keep the faith?" Does a situation bring your faith to a conscious level where you realize it is there? Have you possessed your faith since you were young? Is it something you feel you have to believe to live your life, or do you possess it by conviction and truth?

Faith is everywhere inside our beings. We all have faith albeit on different levels or extremes, but it is present. How many close accidents in your life have you had where you thought you were going to be injured or die? You survived, but have no idea how you managed to escape the situation. Have you thought that something bigger was going on within yourself that had an effect on the outcome? You may have thought that luck was with you, but rather than luck being the primary thought, didn't faith help you through? How many accidents have you personally avoided while driving or crossing the street where you put faith in your own driving or the driving of others? Injuries and fatalities happen every day, but people still drive and walk in the streets. We put faith in ourselves and others. Without faith, would you want to risk injury or death on the roadway?

Faith is possessed by all. We live by faith. It is what keeps us going. We hope that we are exempt from any unfortunate critical situation, but we know it could happen. We know it is possible that something could happen, but we do not change our lives. We dare for the unthinkable to happen and believe it will happen to someone else but not to ourselves.

Faith is a wonderful thing to possess. It keeps life enjoyable. With faith, we can enjoy what we have and nurture what we desire. I live every day with faith in the forefront of my thinking. I believe that things happen for a reason and we are to ponder the situation and outcome in an attempt to learn from it whether the outcome is negative or positive. By having faith, I am led to a greater sense of joy and fulfillment. Though I have experienced negative outcomes, I take from those experiences and learn from them.

We can learn from negative situations and use them to increase our quality of life. It is not difficult to have faith. If we give ourselves to the Lord, then we can give the Lord those worries. We do not need to be burdened with them. How many times do we worry about things? If one of those worries did occur, it would probably be something we could handle. By not consuming ourselves with these negative thoughts, we can find ourselves experiencing increased quality of life. A fair amount of people consume their thoughts with negativity. By giving our worrisome thoughts to the Lord, we are released from them. We are free to think about increasing our quality of life in every way.

Many people have faith and know what it is like to possess faith. There are those who have a more difficult time of letting things go and releasing themselves from these burdens. Which provides a better life: holding on or releasing the burdens? Quality of life can be increased when we realize the presence of faith. Our lives can be affected in a positive way if we are aware of our faith levels. Our faith levels can be strong or waver. Now is the time to discover our doubts.

If we didn't have any faith at all, we would never leave the house. Everyone has some level of faith. We need to think about our levels of faith. Some days do we believe and other days we think the worst things will happen? We should try to have faith every day. Our faith should not waver, and our trust in the Lord should be firm and unshakable. Faith is a belief and trust in God, knowing that God is real even though we can't see Him. The faith in God is where the foundation of faith comes. Once we truly believe that God is our provider, we put faith in His hands. We place our trust in God to give us peace and comfort, and He will rid us of our burdens.

Scriptures are extremely important because they are central to what faith is and what we receive from possessing the faith. If we lose faith, we are able to recover by reading scriptures. Scriptures are powerful and will move people to where God wants them to be. When we fall, the scriptures will pick us up. The scriptures define faith and articulate the rewards and riches we receive.

The following scriptures from the New International Version of the Holy Bible provide evidence of what faith can do for our lives. With faith, we believe in something we cannot see nor touch. Faith can conquer so much for us if we choose to believe.

> See, he is puffed up; his desires are not upright—
> but the righteous will live by his faith. (Habakkuk
> 2:4)

He replied, "Because you have so little faith. I tell you the truth, if you have faith as small as a mustard seed, you can say to this mountain, 'Move from here to there' and it will move. Nothing will be impossible for you." (Matthew 17:20–21)

When Jesus heard this, he was amazed at him, and turning to the crowd following him, he said, "I tell you, I have not found such great faith even in Israel." Then the men who had been sent returned to the house and found the servant well. (Luke 7:9–10)

For in the gospel a righteousness from God is revealed, a righteousness that is by faith from first to last, just as it is written: "The righteous will live by faith." (Romans 1:17)

This righteousness from God comes through faith in Jesus Christ to all who believe. There is no difference, for all have sinned and fall short of the glory of God. (Romans 3:22–23)

If I have the gift of prophecy and can fathom all mysteries and all knowledge, and if I have a faith that can move mountains, but have not love, I am nothing. (1 Corinthians 13:2)

Therefore we are always confident and know that as long as we are at home in the body we are away from the Lord. We live by faith, not by sight. (2 Corinthians 5:6–7)

In addition to all this, take up the shield of faith, with which you can extinguish all the flaming arrows of the evil one. (Ephesians 6:16)

I lift up my eyes to the hills—where does my help come from? My help comes from the Lord, the Maker of heaven and earth. He will not let your foot slip—he who watches over you will not slumber; indeed, he who watches over Israel will neither slumber nor sleep. The Lord watches over you—the Lord is your shade at your right hand; the sun will not harm you by day, nor the moon by night. The Lord will keep you from all harm—he will watch over your life; the Lord will watch over your coming and going both now and forevermore. (Psalm 121:1–8)

Now faith is being sure of what we hope for and certain of what we do not see. By faith we understand that the universe was formed at God's command, so that what is seen was not made out of what was visible. By faith he was commended as a righteous man, when God spoke well of his offerings. And by faith he still speaks, even though he is dead. By faith Enoch was taken from this life, so that he did not experience death; he could not be found, because God had taken him away. For before he was taken, he was commended as one who pleased God, because anyone who comes to him must believe that he exists and that he rewards those who earnestly seek him. By faith Noah, when warned about things not yet seen, in holy fear built an ark to save his family. By faith Abraham, when called to go to a place he would later receive as his inheritance, obeyed and went, even though he did not know where he was going. By faith he made his home in the promised land like a stranger in a foreign country; he lived in tents, as did Isaac and Jacob, who were heirs with him of the same promise. All these people were still living by faith when they died. They did not receive the things promised; they only saw them and welcomed them from a distance. And they admitted that they were aliens and strangers on earth. People who say such things show that they are looking for a country they had left, they would have had opportunity to return. Instead, they were longing for a better country—a heavenly one. Therefore God is not ashamed to be called their God, for he has prepared a city for them. He who had received the promises was about to sacrifice his one and only son, even though God had said to him, "It is through Isaac that your offspring will be reckoned." Abraham reasoned that God could raise the dead, and figuratively speaking, he did receive

Isaac back from death. By faith Moses' parents hid him for three months after he was born, because they saw he was no ordinary child, and they were not afraid of the king's edict. By faith the people passed through the Red Sea as on dry land; but when the Egyptians tried to do so, they were drowned. By faith the walls of Jericho fell, after the people had marched around them for seven days. By faith the prostitute Rehab, because she welcomed the spies, was not killed with those who were disobedient. Women received back their dead, raised to life again. Others were tortured and refused to be released, so that they might gain a better resurrection. Some faced jeers and flogging, while still others were chained and put in prison. They were stoned; they were sawed in two; they were put to death by the sword. These were all commended for their faith, yet none of them received what had been promised. God had planned something better for us so that only together with us would they be made perfect. (excerpted from Hebrews 11:1–39)

Faith has helped me overcome obstacles in my life that would not have been possible. If we have doubt in our minds, we should look at the benefits of faith. We do not have anything to lose and so much to gain. Do we really want to risk not knowing how our quality of life could be improved?

Prayer is a personal event, a private interaction between God and that person. Whether prayer is done privately or in a group setting is not an issue, but rather is prayer in your life? Prayer is connected to faith and a vital part of the overall connection to God. Prayer is similar to faith in some aspects. Our prayer may be answered, and it may be answered in a short period of time or a longer period of time. We may not always know if a prayer is successful. We have faith that our prayer is going to be answered, and through faith we do not need to have proof of our prayer being answered.

Through faith, we know our prayer is heard by the Lord and, in due time, is responded to. Through faith, we also continue to pray even though we may feel our prayer was not answered. Our prayers cannot be measured nor quantified, but our faith doesn't allow our minds to question.

Our purpose in life is always known to God but not necessarily known to us. If we are not always looking to see God's plan for us, we won't receive the message. We always need to be ready to receive God's plan. We may have thought about giving up on God, but we know that God has never given up on us. If our prayers stop, God does not stop His plan for us. He has faith in us regardless of what we do or don't do. We may not be thinking of God, but He is always thinking about us and watching over us for our safety, peace, and comfort.

Prayer is powerful and is heard by God regardless of where we do it and whether it is out loud or silent. Scriptures show that prayer is important in our lives. God's will is for us to pray and be thankful for everything in our lives.

The following scriptures from the New International Version of the Holy Bible show the power of prayers, God's will, and what we receive from continuous prayer. These scriptures can be a focus for us in our lives.

> When I shut up the heavens so that there is no rain, or command locusts to devour the land or send a plague among my people, if my people, who are called by my name, will humble themselves and pray and seek my face and turn from their wicked ways, then will I hear from heaven and will forgive their sin and will heal their land. (2 Chronicles 7:13–14)

> And when you pray, do not be like the hypocrites, for they love to pray standing in the synagogues and on the street corners to be seen by men. I tell you the truth, they have received their reward in full. But when you pray, go into your room, close the door and pray to your Father, who is unseen. Then your Father, who sees what is done in secret, will reward you. And when you pray, do not keep on babbling like pagans, for they think they will be heard because of their many words. Do not be like them, for your Father knows why you need before you ask Him. (Matthew 6:5–8)

> In the same way, the Spirit helps us in our weakness. We do not know what we ought to pray for, but the Spirit himself intercedes for us with groans that words cannot express. And he who searches our hearts knows the mind of the Spirit,

because the Spirit intercedes for the saints in accordance with God's will. (Romans 8:26–27)

Be joyful always, pray continually; give thanks in all circumstances, for this is God's will for you in Christ Jesus. (1 Thessalonians 5:16–18)

The Lord knows what we want and our weaknesses even before we pray for guidance and direction. He works through and within us even if we are not aware of it. If we wait patiently for our answers to come from our prayers, then we will be rewarded. Prayers are heard in any circumstance whether silent or out loud. In any form or fashion, prayers are very powerful and moving.

Prayer is a vital and critical process to be connected with the Lord. I challenge you to pray often and frequently leaving no request out. Wait patiently for your answers, and do not become frustrated. Do not lose trust in the Lord and what He can accomplish for you in your life. The Lord is always there for you in good and bad times. In the good times, thank the Lord for what He has provided, and in the bad times, put your trust in the Lord. The tough times are where you pray for certain things and to get through. Although it is difficult, there is comfort and peace in knowing the Lord has heard your prayer requests. You want to remain strong and receive that strength from the Lord, for the Lord is covering you with hope and a brighter future. Place your situation in the Lord's hands, and see your life be rewarded in a positive light. When you are weak, then the Lord will provide you with strength and power.

Wouldn't it be great to feel that strength and power beyond what we are capable of possessing ourselves? There is so much to be said for the extra lift in life that we feel every day. I pray in private and in a group setting, and I pray for myself and others. I ask for the Lord's guidance when I might be drifting off His path, but I also pray for the great things He has put in my life.

Many people are turning to the Lord. There is something happening in the world, and it is having a huge effect across the country. It is being done by those who are spreading God's message, and God is working through them to reach thousands of people who are finding their lives refreshed and energized. God is using His disciples to carry this mission out en masse, leaving no one untouched. These people are seeing a new life, a life of purpose and meaning with unconditional love, peace, comfort, and direction.

Take the time to think about the following questions, and think about where God fits in your life.

Where is the Lord in your life right now?

_____

Where is prayer in your life?

_____

Where is the faith in your life?

_____

Do you associate with people who have the Lord in their lives? Yes___ No___

Do you openly let people know you believe?
Yes___ No___

Do you believe your prayers are being answered?
Yes___ No___

Do you pray in only the worst times and not the good times? Yes___ No___

When was the first time you became a Christian?

_____

Do you feel that extra lift that God provides?
Yes___ No___

Do you turn to God for peace, comfort, grace, and direction? Yes___ No___

Do you believe that God has a plan for you? Yes___ No___

Do you pray in private and also in group settings?
Yes___ No___

Can you recall the times God has come through for you? Yes___ No___

Do you feel your prayers are going unanswered?
Yes___ No___

Are you involved in any ministries spreading God's plan? Yes___ No___

Do you put your faith in God all of the time?
Yes___ No___

If you are not a believer, this is a life-changing decision. If you are a believer, this will keep you where you should be. Even as you are thinking, the Lord knows your thoughts and is working within you. It is not by chance that you are in His plan because we are all in His plan and the Father leaves no one out.

Do not be afraid to ask the Lord into your life. Do not hesitate to act on what you really want to do. The Lord is waiting for you to accept Him into your life and be free. Experience the joy and celebrate, for you will never walk alone. You will always have company, and you no longer need to fear. Even in darkness, the Lord will show you the way out. The Lord will comfort you, guide you, and give you peace through your life and even thereafter. What a relief to know that you have never been alone. All you need to do is ask Him in and wait for Him to shower you with all that He has to give. It is not too late to decide. The Lord will welcome you with open arms and His love, which you will never experience from anyone else. Remember, this love is forever and is unconditional. His love for you will not waver nor decrease.

Now it is time for you to ask Him in. Do not hesitate nor delay this action. You will now experience life in a new and exciting way. Enjoy the journey through life with the Lord. You have been awakened and energized for what you are about to receive from the Lord.

FIVE

PROCESS

You have many times thought about your success and how exactly you will get there. First you must have a process in place and then a strong mind to complete the process. The process must entail an environment in which your chances of success are high. This environment is where your mind is always in a mode of moving forward versus backward. This process is one where your objective is accomplished. The process therein must not only consist of how to get there but also entail always being in a position of experiencing success. The position of success lies in your mind being conditioned to be hungry for success.

The phrases listed in chapter 6 will keep your mind stimulated. These are instrumental in conditioning your mind to be at the highest energy level. These phrases and the ones you may think of will increase your drive for success. This will work for you if you use the phrases daily. Make it something you follow through on. Throughout the day, your mind will stay on track. It is a known fact that the more positive you are, the more accomplishments you will encounter. You have what it takes to succeed, and you know what is needed as well to succeed.

You need to do this because the media, whether it's paper or television, is portraying negative rather than positive events. We often do not see nor hear about the success stories of someone but rather the wrongs of individuals. This can cause people to decrease their drive and motivation as this information further sinks into the mind. I often have wondered why the media is not more focused on what people do right. You cannot let the negativity in the media affect your drive for success. There are thousands of success stories, but we just do not hear about them. Maybe the day will come when we can see a success story as the front page news in the papers or the lead story on the television. Unfortunately the media is not a big help in accomplishing and fulfilling your dreams.

You may want to put a phrase daily on an index card. Carry the card with you, and look at it whenever you can. Keep it in the car in a place where you can see it. This will no doubt increase your drive for success. The more you read the phrases, the more you will see a difference in your thinking. Your mind will continue to increase in positive thinking. The phrases will be memorized after time, and you can simply recall them any time you wish. This is part of conditioning your mind to think the way you want versus allowing other things such as the media to influence your thoughts.

I encourage you to think of action phrases that move you. The ones in this book are what I have collected over time. Certain words can move a person to action more than others. You know the ones that put a smile on your face and inspire you to greater things. I challenge you to do this and see the difference. Notice the smile on your face when you say certain words or think of specific events. Use this to nurture your thinking process. This will build your confidence without your necessarily having to work at it. We can smile many times a day without putting any work or effort into it. Log the times you smile, and realize your thinking is positive. Use this as a tool you have at your disposal to increase your ability to make things happen.

Life is not always easy, but we can get out of life what we desire if we have the drive, motivation, desire, and confidence to succeed.

This is the process to use in thinking about your short-term goals, which are goals you are able to achieve within a month or two.

Step 1: Complete the self-reflection exercises.

The self-reflection exercises are found in chapter 3. They will help you think about where you want to go. The exercises will help you in seeing where your strengths and interests are. Self-reflection exercises are designed to help you look at yourself and inventory your life—past and present.

Step 2: Review the phrases.

You can find these throughout the book. Review them all, and see which ones draw your interest more. Maybe you will think of one on your own. These phrases are meant to inspire you and provide you with inspiration and motivation. The phrases are positive and will move you to an "I can do it" atti-tude. Some of them will definitely inspire you more than others.

Step 3: Write down realistic goals for the month.

You should be inspired and motivated by reading the phrases, and your mind should be in a mode to produce results in thinking what you can accomplish in the short term. Believe in yourself, and see your confidence increase. Your goals are yours, set by you and defined by you. They are your only means to set yourself up for success.

Step 4: Pick out phrases to define in a month.

You may also think of your own phrases. The phrases listed in this book are the ones that I have thought of over the years. It would be more beneficial and moving if you think of some yourself. Decide which ones really strike you and get you thinking. These phrases are meant to reenergize you. They are meant to give you feeling and attitude that you can do it. These phrases will continue to keep you in a positive mood.

Step 5: Write down what the phrases mean to you.

Think about this for awhile. Let it really sink in and take hold. This will be crucial in moving ahead and reaching your goals. You have already reviewed the phrases and picked the ones that inspired you the most. Now what does this phrase mean to you? How does it inspire you? Why does this put a smile on your face? How does this phrase give you a positive attitude? This will only reinforce your positive thinking and success. Continue to build your own positive thinking by reinforcing your core thinking.

Step 6: Refer back to your worksheets periodically.

If you feel disconnected from your plan, it is time to get reenergized and focused. Hopefully, you will refer back to your worksheets often enough so you won't get off track. The process is encompassed in such a way that you should be set for success.

Step 7: Rate your progress at the end of each month.

Analyze your progress, and make sure you are on pace to achieve your goals. You are evolving as you continue your life journey. Your progress is an indication of your dedication and commitment to your goals. Monitoring your progress keeps you focused and your mind actively engaged. You will aspire to greater accomplishments as you continue finishing your short-term goals. Short-term goals completed will lead to long-term goals success.

SIX

PHRASES

These phrases listed below are ones that I have thought of over time. You can use these phrases to motivate and inspire you. You can think of your own and add them to increase your motivation. Continually use these phrases to complete your goals and objectives. When you think you cannot do something, use these phrases to tell yourself, "Yes, you can do it." Likewise, when you know you are on the path to success use these phrases to keep you going and keep that motivation alive and energized. Do not underestimate what these phrases or your own can do for you. Continue to work your plan of success with the inclusion of these phrases.

1. The sun can motivate us—look at the brightness.

2. Tomorrow isn't here—today is. What's your plan?

3. Are you smiling? Something is there to smile about.

4. Success comes from failures—what have you learned?

5. Be positive—be happy—be the best you can be.

6. We can accomplish anything—regardless of age or any other factors.

7. What's your dream? Live it—plan—don't let it stop.

8. Don't stop—put yourself in drive—reach your destination.

9. Inspire yourself—smile—observe what happens.

10. If you are happy, be assured others will see that.

11. Walk like your dream is close to fulfillment.

12. Think about it—chances increase of it happening.

13. Guess what? You are capable of making it happen.

14. Make notes. Don't let your dream get away.

15. This is your life—use it wisely.

16. Happiness is everywhere—you just have to look.

17. At the end of the day, look—you have made progress.

18. The stars can look so bright—just as our dreams can be.

19. Plan your success in stages, and reward yourself.

20. If you start with small steps, big steps will follow.

21. No need to convince yourself you can do it.

22. Just do it, and reap the benefits and rewards.

23. A smile lets everyone know where you stand.

24. What do you really want? Plan to get it.

25. You are special. Look at all the ways.

26. Life is as precious as you are. Are you living it?

27. Life is right in front of you. Do you see it?

28. Do you think life has passed you by? Time for reflection.

29. A positive attitude will keep you bearing the great fruits of life.

30. Change is only a heartbeat away. Positive change inspires and motivates.

31. Face your fear, and tomorrow will be brighter.

32. Constant worry only takes happiness from you. Who wins?

33. You have the drive to make it happen.

34. Insight—knowing what you want and how to get it.

35. Let your thoughts inspire and move you.

36. Count the ways in which you can prosper.

37. No time like now to know where you are at.

38. Life can be better and within your control.

39. Control is in your grasp—hang on—seize it tightly.

40. Do not put off tomorrow what you are thinking today.

41. Think often and realize your thoughts.

42. Wake up—your dreams need to be fulfilled.

43. Reward yourself for your accomplishments.

44. Reach out—grasp the beauty of life you see.

45. Life is all about where you are and where you are going.

46. Transform yourself and notice the changes.

47. Life is full of ups and downs—increase your ups.

48. Every day can be another step to happiness.

49. Think about what could be if you put your mind to it.

50. Faith will inspire and motivate you.

51. Look ahead—keep walking forward—getting closer to your dreams.

52. Every step you take gets you closer to your dreams.

53. Where are you in your life path?

54. Are you on track to reach your life destination?

55. Your dream is closer than you think.

56. Your dream might appear to be distant—zoom in to take a closer look.

57. Success matters to you, only you.

58. You are in control of your own destiny.

59. Make your day as bright as the sun is shining.

60. Every day is another chance to fulfill your destiny.

61. Each day provides warmth for us with the sun rising.

62. Inspiration, motivation, and drive all come from within.

63. Be aware of what you are consciously thinking.

64. Any step big or small will drive and move you.

65. Don't think about how large the step is, just move forward.

66. Just think, just imagine, and some day it will be within reach.

67. No matter where you are in life, everything is possible.

68. Be confident, inspire yourself, and watch yourself move.

69. Challenges are meant to be faced with hope and faith.

70. Meet your challenges, and conquer with decisiveness.

71. By self-reflection, you will see your true strengths.

72. Instill action words to motivate you to victory.

73. Condition your mind to accept only positive responses.

74. Look at the stars, and capture your dream.

75. Success is not accomplished without failures along the way.

76. Staying calm and focused gives structure to your being.

77. The finish line is only a few hurdles away and waiting.

78. Don't accept less than what you desire.

79. Look at all the opportunities in life. Which one is your real dream?

80. Plan your every step, and direct yourself to the ultimate goal.

81. What have you noticed lately that brings a smile to your face?

82. Dreams are not realized without planning, thinking, and strategy.

83. Set aside some quiet time, and set your thoughts on fire.

84. Find your place to think, and set your mind free.

85. Your passion is still inside of you and waiting to surface.

86. You have special gifts waiting to be discovered.

87. You are special in your own way. Have you found the gift?

88. Achieve your dream through discovery and awareness.

89. Search for and rescue your dream.

90. Attitude is a major component of success.

91. *Perseverance* spells *preserve your victory.*

92. Isn't it amazing what you can do in your life?

93. Live every day to the fullest like there is no tomorrow.

94. Decide what you really want, then condition your mind to retrieve it.

95. Walk the path that you find victory on.

96. The future can be defined to your specifications.

97. Define your dream in the brightest form possible.

98. Stay true to your heart, and listen to it.

99. Flexibility is energizing in life. Where can you step out and see the world in a different perspective? Picking up a new character trait might be one place to start.

100. The light keeps getting brighter as you get to the destination.

101. Coordinate your heart and mind to excel in your vision.

102. Don't lose yourself in the midst of victory.

103. Seize the moment, and live for now.

104. Exercise your mind, and imagine the possibilities.

105. Tell yourself you are worthy of your dreams.

106. Promise yourself never to give up.

107. Just realize how special you are, and move with it.

108. There is no such thing as, "I cannot do it."

109. If you believe in yourself, look at what life gives you back.

110. We only have one life to live—make the most of it.

111. Rejoice in who you are, then share that with others.

112. Getting to the top of the mountain is tough, but look at the view once you are there.

113. Every one of us makes this world a better place to live.

114. Your contribution to this world is unfinished.

115. Isn't it beautiful how you can add happiness to your life.

116. Success is within reach—you can see the moment arriving to rejoice.

117. Think often about your accomplishments and goals.

118. Give a hug to someone you love, and feel the sensation.

119. Don't look behind and miss what's in front of you.

120. Let yourself go, and believe in yourself every minute.

121. You have potential to achieve your dreams and goals.

122. Life is a learning experience every single day.

123. Greater things are waiting to happen in your life.

124. Listen to your heart, and follow the signs.

125. Look for the signs in your life that inspire and motivate you.

126. Have fun achieving your goals.

127. Your pursuit for increased happiness is waiting to happen.

128. Nothing is more satisfying than rejoicing in your happiness.

129. Seize the moment, and rejoice in what you have.

130. Keep accomplishments on your mind to motivate you.

131. Think of the last time you rejoiced and how good it felt.

132. Don't be surprised at what you can accomplish—you are always capable of it.

133. Look at what the world can offer you—then go for it nonstop.

134. The mind will go anywhere you want it; just focus and pick your target.

135. Place yourself in the best position to win.

136. Attitude isn't something. It's everything, and the difference is overwhelming.

137. Keep the passion alive, and you will experience the reward.

138. Keep the love flowing at the maximum level, and watch your heart.

139. Make a difference in your life—it is never too late.

140. Remember, it's your life to change for the better.

141. Your purpose in life continues to unfold and move you to greater things.

142. It should not surprise you of what your mind is capable of.

143. You are unique in such a way that sets you apart from everyone else.

144. Keep your mind moving forward with creative, inspiring ideas.

145. This world is continually being built on new ideas—it could be yours.

146. Keep building yourself up by adding the necessary ingredients to finish the job.

147. Develop your own strategy for the outcome you desire.

148. Happiness is yours if you believe in yourself.

149. Your desires are the path to greater expectations of yourself.

150. Commit your life to a journey of dreams, desires, and happiness.

151. You can achieve great things just as much as anyone else.

152. Your life is here, it's now, it's moving, not letting you get off.

153. Feel the power you have and increase it—energize yourself to the next phase.

154. Fill your mind with maximum vision, always seeing your dreams and believing.

155. Look at the choices—so many of them—which ones inspire and move you?

156. Only slow down to see how much closer you are to your dreams.

157. You are the gatekeeper of what goes in and out of your mind—take charge.

158. Life is full of simple pleasures. What are yours?

159. Even when it's cloudy, there is sun. Where is your sunshine?

160. What are all of the dreams you have ever thought of?

161. Every day you can be thankful for something. What is it for you today?

162. The best message you ever get is listening to your heart. What is it telling you?

163. Life is too precious for any happiness to escape—so grab it now.

164. Search and retain the positive thoughts in your mind. Destroy the rest.

165. Faith will inspire and guide you to the finish line despite any obstacles.

166. Put your mind to it—apply your strategy—focus on the outcome.

167. You deserve happiness in your life, but you need to ask for it and know what you are looking for.

168. Continue strong on the offensive, and you will meet less resistance.

169. If you believe in your positive self-talk and continually reinforce it, you will succeed.

170. You will never realize your potential unless you set your mind to it.

171. Express yourself now. What do you want?

172. Realizing your potential will be one of your greatest accomplishments.

173. Continue to nurture your gift and skill to expose your real talents.

174. It is your decision to decide what your life story will be at the end.

175. There is no end unless there is a beginning.

176. The foundation of your being rests in your faith, hope, and dreams.

177. Always remember where you are going and your route of passage.

178. There is so much more you know than you will ever discover and realize in your lifetime.

179. There is no question that you are meant to succeed. Do you see it? Keep looking.

180. There is no better satisfaction in life than to feel and enjoy happiness each and every single day.

181. What are your landmarks to know you are on course?

182. Keep searching continuously, listening to your heart until you find your purpose, and when you do, you will know it.

183. Find your special place where you find your thoughts continuously flowing.

184. You will have more to show for your life if you focus more on what you are going to become than in why you have been.

185. Communicate your dreams and wishes to yourself. You will hear them louder coming from yourself.

186. Change can happen anytime, anyplace, and anywhere along your life journey.

187. Look up, and as the sun rises, you too will rise and shine with a new beginning.

188. As you pass through life, continue to fill yourself up with things that increase your happiness until the end.

189. Keep in touch—remind yourself continuously of what your desires are.

190. There is no guarantee to life longevity so make the most of what there is, knowing you enjoy the fullness of every day.

191. Enjoy the time now, and rejoice in your blessings.

192. Your wish should be your desire, and your heart should be your driving. *Desire and drive* spells *completion and mission accomplished.*

193. This is your life. Take control now, and manage your destiny.

194. Your dream is yours only and always with you.

195. Confidence, persistence, motivation, and drive will result in success.

196. Accomplishments today will result in greater success tomorrow.

197. The rising of the sun represents a new and fresh beginning.

198. The only magic in success is your believing in yourself.

199. Dream and realize that success is closer than you think.

200. Understanding and knowing how to condition your mind is half the battle.

201. Saying *yes* and *I can* will go a long way in defining yourself.

202. Put strategy in your life, and play to win on your terms.

203. Success can mean different things to a person. What does it mean for you?

204. It only matters what success means to you.

205. Concentrate on what your mission is and your means of reaching that.

206. Love is everywhere. You just need to search your heart and find it.

207. Life is short—live it—live it to the fullest.

208. The brightness is always ahead, not behind.

209. Eternal love is unconditional love.

210. Reach out and live your life.

211. Anything can happen if you have the will.

212. If you drive fast to your goal, the outcome will be sooner.

213. Live for today, and enjoy what is at the moment.

214. Let your heart lead you to the fruit.

215. The beauty of the nature will free your mind.

216. Success is within reach—plan for it today and now.

217. Imagine what you could have, and then receive it.

218. Plan what you want to happen, and have fun getting there.

219. Think about what you want, and then plan and watch it appear.

220. Will power will get you places—keep the drive alive.

221. Your mind can work for you if you condition it.

222. Thoughts can keep your dreams alive—don't stop.

223. Being positive will get you everywhere—just imagine.

224. Think for the moment; enjoy the moment right now.

225. Everything is within reach if you truly want it.

226. Your success is only a heartbeat away.

227. Smiling can be contagious. Experience the good feeling by seeing the smile and giving the smile.

228. Happiness in life is for our taking if we desire it.

229. Be happy within yourself, and hear what others say.

230. The moment is now—right now—to smile and live.

231. You are your worst enemy—plan for the destruction.

232. In life, you can only move forward and learn from the past.

233. Joy can be expressed and felt in many ways. Where is your joy?

234. Measure yourself up to your own abilities and potential, not anyone else's.

235. When you see the light at the end of the tunnel, your dreams and goals are starting to be realized.

236. Your potential is unknown until you discover it.

237. Be thankful for what you have, and be yearning for what is to come.

238. Envision your success, and permanently place that within your mind with access twenty-four hours a day.

239. Time is on your side unless you choose otherwise. Have you chosen to use time to your advantage before the game clock expires?

240. Learn to outsmart your negative self-talk, and feel the difference in every way. Track your daily positive progress.

241. Let creativity ignite your brain and set it on fire. Log all the creations you have.

242. Guess what? It's your turn to inventory your mind. What is there today?

243. What is your passion? Bring it alive today.

244. Live in the present and now. Where is your joy?

245. Positive things happen every day. Open your mind, hunt within, and you will find them. Where are they? Rejoice.

246. _____

247. _____

248. _____

249. _____

250. _____

SEVEN

MONTHLY PLAN

Having a monthly plan to guide you is critical to your success. Your monthly plan may be completed in a month or may be part of a long-term plan. You want to incorporate the phrases found in chapter 6 with your monthly goals found in this chapter. Throughout the month, refer to your goals and reflect on the phrases you have already listed or pick another one and reflect on a new one.

Staying on track is not always easy. Your success is dependent upon your plan for staying on track. Many times you can find yourself diverted from your plan, and the farther you get off track the tougher it is to get back. Your goal will be easier to meet by staying on track the whole time. The phrases are a component of your road to success.

Think of yourself as being on a railroad track. You are on the track going at your own speed. You are not required to exit at any point unless you do so on your own. You will have along the way various distractions that could put you on another path. Think of the things that could make you exit. Be prepared and ready to face those things before you see them. You are always able to get back on the track, but why get off if you don't need to? With a railroad track, there is always a beginning and an end with many exits in between. Some of the exits you make are out of your control, such as medical situations. The exits I want you to think about are the ones in your control. There is no need to stop on the track, but it is easy to do. You want to push yourself as fast as you can because most likely no one is pushing you from behind. You are in total control of where you want to go and how fast you want to arrive.

Life is a journey that only you live for and enjoy. Where are you on your railroad track? Things that happen in your life could cross your track and either derail you or have no impact on your journey. Enhance your chances of staying on track by making the decision beneficial to your plan. The phrases assist you in keeping the focus on your journey.

List all of the goals regardless of how important or involved they are. Keep in mind that accomplishment of any goals is a stepping stone to larger goals and builds your confidence level.

Date: _____   **Month:** _____

Monthly Goals:

1. _____

2. _____

3. _____

4. _____

Some goals will be listed continuously if you are still working on them. Have a mixture of goals that will be short term, which will be completed within a few months.

Phrase: _____

_____

What does it mean to you?

_____

_____

Phrase: _____

_____

What does it mean to you?

_____

_____

Phrase: _____

_____

What does it mean to you?

_____

_____

Phrase: _____

_____

What does it mean to you?

_____

_____

List some ways you will accomplish your goals.

1. _____

2. _____

3. _____

4. _____

5. _____

6. _____

7. _____

8. _____

9. _____

10. _____

List some of the positive things that have happened to you.

1. _____

2. _____

3. _____

4. _____

5. _____

6. _____

7. _____

8. _____

9. _____

10. _____

EIGHT

MONTHLY REVIEW

Monthly reviews of ongoing goals are a must do, but just as critical is a review of what went right and wrong. This includes taking into account your mood, which is a variable that affects your progress.

This chapter lays out the foundation to track your success and failure at making appropriate changes. Were your expectations met to the fullest? If not, then you need to further dissect the way and method you used to increase and satisfy your expectations. Do not feel you cannot reach that milestone if you fell short. Remember Abraham Lincoln who failed more than forty times before he tasted success. Lincoln is an inspiration to all of us that success can follow failure no matter how many times failure happens.

This chapter also entails reflecting on your feelings. Feelings affect your level of success, as does your attitude. You are asked if your attitude was gloomy or bright in the last month. If your attitude was gloomy, then you want to find out why. If your month was gloomy, then your level of accomplishment was lower. If you felt great, then the energy was present and your drive for success was enhanced. You then want to keep that momentum going.

If you are aware of your feelings as much as possible, then you are always in a position to change them for the better. Likewise, if you know change is possible, then you have more insight in being aware of the effect feelings have on your life.

Feelings and moods can be different at any time and vary in length. The key that you possess is your knowledge to know change can happen. Once you realize this, then the door opens for you to reach your destination. The control is yours, and the question really is, "What do you really want to accomplish in life?" It is no longer a matter of if it can happen but only a matter of when it happens.

Date: _____   **Month:** _____

Did you meet your expectations?

_____

Now is the time to review your progress on your goals.

Remember, not all goals need to be fulfilled for you to feel good about yourself. Any steps forward will bring forth larger steps later.

How would you rate your level of accomplishment for the month?

Low ___   **Medium** ___   **High** ___

List your greatest accomplishments for the month.

1. _____

2. _____

3. _____

4. _____

5. _____

6. _____

How would you rate your attitude?

Gloomy ___   **Bright** ___

Circle the positive feelings you experienced in the last month.

Love	Adored	Tender	Caring
Affectionate	Friendly	Alive	Vibrant
Happy	Great	Proud	Capable
Independent	Excited	Patient	Strong
Alert	Amused	Relaxed	Content
Comfortable	Wanted	Worthy	Admired
Pity	Empathy	Secure	Peaceful
Determined	Attractive	Sure	Elated
Eager	Joyful	Glad	Satisfied
Optimistic	Courageous	Trusted	Relieved
Warm	Brave	Daring	Effective
Superior	Adequate	Helpful	Respected

Describe your best feelings for the month.

_____

_____

_____

How will you keep that feeling alive? List ways that will bring that feeling to you again.

_____

_____

_____

Circle the negative feelings you experienced in the last month.

Unpopular	Suspicious	Discontented	Disappointed
Dissatisfied	Tempted	Envious	Disgusted
Frustrated	Perplexed	Impatient	Unhappy
Despised	Depressed	Dejected	Bored
Bad	Sad	Helpless	Useless
Worthless	Abandoned	Alienated	Timid
Worried	Paid	Unsure	Guilty
Hopeless	Mad	Scared	Trapped
Alarmed	Accused	Defeated	Stupid
Afraid	Aggressive	Inferior	Tense
Troubled	Anxious		

Describe your worst feelings for the month.

_____

_____

_____

_____

_____

_____

What are you going to do to decrease the frequency of that feeling?

_____

_____

_____

_____

_____

_____

_____

NINE

ANNUAL REVIEW

Look through your monthly plans, and note what you have accomplished. Remember to stay positive. If you didn't complete a goal, it is an opportunity for you to grow. This is your chance to broaden your horizons in so many ways. It is always beneficial to start a new year off with short-term and long-term goals. I would recommend doing the annual review at the end of each year, even if you have gone only several months. Many have done their resolutions for the year. Great idea. This keeps you looking to the future on a positive and encouraging note.

What were your greatest accomplishments for the year?

1. _____

2. _____

3. _____

4. _____

5. _____

6. _____

7. _____

8. _____

9. _____

What will you do differently in the next year? State your comments in a positive fashion.

1. _____

2. _____

3. _____

4. _____

5. _____

6. _____

7. _____

8. _____

9. _____

Now go through the self-reflection exercises again and see what has changed. Look at any differences in your answers, and draft a plan to improve on areas needed. This is your chance to look and see where you can make a difference for the next year. This is important to review to keep you focused and grow as a person. Always remember you are a work in progress. You are growing every day in areas of your life and of your choosing. You are growing even if you consciously are not aware of it.

Review your short-term goals. Are you satisfied with your success? List your short-term goals you wish to accomplish in the next month or two.

1. _____

2. _____

3. _____

4. _____

5. _____

6. _____

7. _____

8. _____

9. _____

Review your long-term goals. Are you satisfied with your success? List your long-term goals you wish to accomplish in the next year. These are goals that will take several months to years to complete.

1. _____

2. _____

3. _____

4. _____

5. _____

6. _____

7. _____

8. _____

9. _____

I hope it has been another successful year for you. It was a year in which you saw positive things happen. It was also a year in which you saw places grow or things change. A year in review is rewarding and beneficial for what will happen the next year. At year's end, try to come up with resolutions for the following year. Just write them down as you think of them. You then can plan these out as short-term or long-term goals. Resolutions are a good way to start out the new year. How you overcome failure to meet success determines your final destination. Failure is a temporary obstacle that you learn from and that helps you get back on the track to success.

Your last year was a journey that consisted of many events and challenges. You made your best decisions at the time you needed to and sharpened your decision-making thought process. Every decision, right or wrong, has improved your insight into how you make decisions. Most decisions are made with some thought, and sometimes the wrong one is made. Sometimes wrong decisions can be corrected without any major damage and consequences. Do not fear making decisions, but rather let it provide you with options and open doors for you. It also puts your mind in position to do some thinking, which is necessary for you to explore what you want in life.

Continue your road to success. Do not give up or give in. Look at decisions as increasing your options, and more doors will open. Some wrong decisions can be corrected. What can you do better in reaching your dreams? Have you thought of other dreams you want to reach? Keep your faith and imagination alive. Imagine your dreams, and picture them in your mind. This is your first step. Now, do you have the faith to see this come to life? If so, then it's only a matter of time until your dreams live. Imagine, dream, and see it happen before your eyes.

TEN

RELAXATION EXERCISES

Relaxation is important to give your mind and body needed rest. Relaxation also reduces the stress you feel and put upon yourself. Stress can be controlled, although it is not necessarily always easy. The key is to find relaxation exercises that work for you. You may have to try different ones to see which ones give you maximum positive results. There are numerous exercises listed in this chapter that could work for you. Check the ones you feel will give you the maximum results. Seize the time you are in these exercises, and think only about relaxing. Free yourself and give yourself permission within, if needed, to truly enjoy relaxing. Do not think about what might be going bad or deadlines. Let those things go, and live for the moment. Feel the peace when you are relaxed. Your mind and body need this relaxation to get filled with that energy and creativity. Without relaxation, you will drain your body of energy and be less productive in reaching your dreams.

Our bodies respond to stress by pumping adrenaline into our systems. This then prepares us for what is referred to as the "fight or flight." In essence your muscles tense up and you are left with a decision. Are you ready to fight or flee for your life?

1. Learn deep breathing exercises. Do this by breathing in for six counts, hold for four counts, expel for six counts. Continue this for as long as you can and to a point where you feel relaxed.

2. Think of something beautiful, something that you have dreamed of or thought of that puts you in a place you wished was real. Think of that with a focus on mind over matter.

3. Read the Bible.

4. Try aerobic exercises. Aerobic is defined as a nonstop, at least twelve minutes, exercise of the muscles in the lower body at a comfortable pace. Attempt to do this for thirty to forty-five minutes each day for five days out of the week. Some aerobic exercises are brisk walking, bicycling, jogging, skating, running, dancing, and distance swimming.

5. Practice yoga.

6. Listen to a tape recording of waterfalls or something equally soothing.

7. Take sleep very seriously. Try not to sleep on the couch. Keep the television off.

8. Set your thermostat in the bedroom between sixty-five and sixty-eight degrees when you are going to bed. Sleeping is much easier when you have cooler temperatures.

9. Use a "quiet do not disturb" sign if need be to remind others not to come in.

10. Avoid exercising before going to sleep. Exercise makes you alert, not sleepy. Exercising before bedtime can interfere with sleep.

11. Meditate.

12. Encourage yourself to enjoy more humor in your life. This includes both your initiating the humor, such as telling jokes and being more witty, and going places where you react to the humor, such as going to comedy clubs. Feel free to let yourself go and give yourself a great belly laugh.

13. Get hypnotized.

14. Acquire a new hobby.

15. Take a walk around the lake, the block, or the park.

16. Observe the stars in the sky, and dream.

17. Think of something funny, and laugh.

18. Write. Move stuff from your head to paper.

19. Take a bath.

20. Sing.

21. Cry.

22. Dance.

23. Read out loud something soothing, relaxing, and funny.

24. Talk to someone who is there only to listen to you.

25. Pray.

26. _____

27. _____

28. _____

29. _____

30. _____

Make notes to yourself below on what your success was like or any other comments to improve on what you are doing. Keep a journal of what is and is not working for you. Continue to pinpoint your areas of relaxation.

_____

_____

_____

_____

_____

Continue to refer to this chapter for your relaxation and ways to reduce stress. Continue to pinpoint what works for you. You now have the tools to start the process. It is your life you are changing to fully enjoy the happiness that resides within yourself. Everyone desires and works toward increasing happiness, and you now have the tools and knowledge to do just that. Don't wait until tomorrow to start this, but now is an ideal time. As we all know, today is the day to make it happen while tomorrow is only another way to put it off.

ELEVEN

INVENTORY YOUR LIFE VARIABLES

Taking an inventory of your life variables is beneficial and critical in enriching your life daily. If you do not find out where you need to go, you will not arrive. If you do not find out which parts of your life need growing, you will find yourself staying in one spot. Daily growing as a person increases happiness in your life. Improvement in how you live provides you with the capacity to live a better life. You can gain insight into where you want your life to be by examining various life variables.

The life variables encompass your life but in different aspects. One aspect of your life might be doing great while another needs improvement. It is no secret that we want to do things differently or better, but it is a matter of knowing what to change. You are always evolving as a person, but you are not always aware of changes taking place. By taking an inventory of your life variables, you know what changes are desired. This chapter is designed to help you evaluate where you are at this moment with your life variables. This is your moment to go deep into your life and engage yourself in this process. Find a place where you can think and change things for the better.

Change can take place in different ways. Behaviors, thinking, and appearance are all different ways of changing. Do not be afraid of change; rather look forward to it. You are evolving, and this should be exciting for you. There are people who will not change, but many of those do not know what to change. If you know what to change and your life would be enhanced, wouldn't you want to change? This chapter will lead you to determine what changes you could make. Now it is up to you to follow through and see it happen.

Think about your values. What values do you have? What values are important for you to have? What values do you wish to acquire?

Answer the questions with each life variable, and assess where you are at. Develop a plan to improve these life variables, which will increase your quality of life. Remember, it is never too late for you to get more out of life and live life every day to the fullest. Life is short, and it is yours to enjoy while you know you can.

FAMILY AND FRIENDS

Are you surrounded by caring, loving family and friends? Yes___ No___

If not, what can you do differently?

_____

_____

Who is your most important friend? Why?

_____

_____

Are you always reaching out to increase your network of friends? Yes___ No___

If not, what can you do differently?

_____

_____

Do you say, "I love you" to family? Yes___ No___

If not, what are you feeling? Why do you think you are unable to say this? What are you going to do differently?

_____

_____

Do you have constant and regular communication with your family? Yes___ No___

If not, what is blocking you from this and what are you going to do differently to improve this?

_____

_____

_____

SPIRITUALITY

Where are you spiritually at this moment?

_____

_____

What does spirituality mean to you?

_____

_____

Are you at peace with your spirituality? Yes___ No___

What would give you additional peace and comfort?

_____

_____

Do you turn to your spirituality in tough times?
Yes___ No___

Do you consider yourself spiritual but not religious?
Yes___ No___

What is the difference for you?

_____

_____

Is your spirituality strong when times are great? Yes
___ No___

RELIGION

Do you consider yourself religious? Yes___ No___

Have you switched from one religion to another? Yes___ No___

If yes, why the switch?

_____

_____

_____

_____

Is your faith stronger being a believer? Yes___ No___

If not, why isn't it? What can be improved?

_____

_____

_____

Are you wanting to be saved? Yes___ No___

Describe your thoughts and feelings on being saved. What does it mean to you?

_____

_____

_____

FINANCES

What are your total expenses? _____

What is your income? _____

Do you feel you need assistance in managing your finances? Yes___ No___

Do you know where your money goes? Yes___ No___

Do you have the power to curb spending if necessary? Yes___ No___

Would it be advantageous for you to see a financial counselor? Yes___ No___

Are you able to meet your expenses? Yes___ No___

What other means of income are available to you?

_____

_____

_____

_____

_____

_____

_____

Are you able to save for retirement? Yes___ No___

SEXUALITY

Is your sexuality at the point you want it? Yes___ No___

Should you increase your sexuality? Is it the right thing? Yes___ No___

Explain your answer. Why is it the right thing to do or not to do?

_____

_____

Have you thought of questions regarding your sexuality? Yes___ No___

If yes, what were your thoughts?

_____

_____

What have you done to put your mind at rest?

_____

_____

What is your level of sexuality now, and is it appropriate for where you are in life?

_____

_____

JOB SECURITY

Do you feel secure in your job? Yes___ No___

Is your job rewarding and enjoyable? Yes___ No___

If need be, what other jobs could you do right now?

_____

_____

_____

_____

_____

_____

What jobs would you want to do that involve further education?

_____

_____

_____

_____

_____

_____

_____

Dreams and Goals

Have any of your dreams been realized yet?
Yes___ No___

What are some of your dreams now?

_____

_____

Are you constantly thinking of your dreams?
Yes___ No___

Where would you be right now if your dreams had come true?

_____

_____

Imagine your dreams. Do you have the faith they will happen? Yes___ No___

Describe your answer.

_____

_____

Do you believe your dreams can come true? Yes___ No___

Describe your answer.

_____

_____

EMOTIONAL WELL-BEING

Are you happy with your life right now? Yes___ No___

Are your emotions running all over the place? Yes___ No___

If yes, what are you feeling right now?

_____

_____

_____

Do you have any health concerns that are a huge burden on your mind? Yes___ No___

If yes, what are they?

_____

_____

_____

What are you doing to improve your emotional well-being?

_____

_____

_____

Do you feel you are waking up refreshed every morning? Yes___ No___

If not, what do you feel like when you do wake up most of the time?

_____

_____

Where are your life variables in your life at the moment? Summarize your current thoughts. What are you thinking?

_____

_____

Now that you have examined the variables in your life, it is time to rate the importance of them. On the next page, in the first column, mark each category with a number between one and ten. The number one represents the lowest rating, signifying you are lacking severely in this category. The number ten indicates you have reached your full maximum potential. This column is designed to see where you are the weakest. This will assist you in knowing where you want to evolve and improve. Were you surprised at what you learned?

In the second column, put the life variables in the order of priority for yourself. The most important life variable would be rated one and the least important life variable would be rated eight. Now, compare the two columns. Have you noticed maybe the least important life variable to you is the one you need improvement on? If this is the case for you, recognize and acknowledge that you may have to work harder to make progress. This is because you have determined this variable not to be important at this point. Making a decision to improve on this life variable requires you to now put importance on this.

	Importance Rating	Priority Rating
	1–10	1–8
Family and Friends	___	___
Spirituality	___	___
Religion	___	___
Finances	___	___
Sexuality	___	___
Job Security	___	___
Dreams and Goals	___	___
Emotional Well-Being	___	___

Now that you have finished rating your life variables, determine which ones you will focus on. You do not want to stop at this point because you know now what to work on. You are on your way to increasing your quality of life by being the best you can be. Your desire and wish to achieve more is in your control. Any obstacles you face can be knocked down and removed.

TWELVE

DREAMS AND GOALS FLOW CHART

This chapter contains a flow chart to assist you in tracking your progress. This chapter will keep you focused on your dreams and goals. This requires you to put thought into what you want to accomplish and when. This chapter gives you a process that you can easily follow. You can reuse these charts over and over.

FLOW CHART

Complete the exercise in Exhibit 1. Use the following instructions to help you complete the chart.

1. List your dreams.

2. Rate them in order of priority.

3. List your strengths and weaknesses.

4. Rate them again after analyzing your strengths and weaknesses.

5. Decide which one has the best chance of success for you. You should have a good idea of where you stand. By completing this exercise, you are planning your success.

6. In one or two sentences, state what you hope to accomplish. This is a promise you are making to yourself.

7. Write the completion date.

8. Plan your objectives in sequence from start to finish on your overall mission.

9. Put in a date that you plan to finish each objective.

10. Put in the date that you completed each objective.

11. Reward yourself for a job well done. You want to make sure the reward is one you strive to reach. If you place a high value on the reward, your aspirations for success will be increased. The reward is something you will work really hard for.

12. Complete the lessons learned section.

Long-term Dreams
Flow Chart

Dreams/ Goals	Rate	Weaknesses/ Strengths	Rate
_____		_____	
_____	___	_____	___
_____		_____	
_____		_____	
		_____	
_____		_____	
_____	___	_____	___
_____		_____	
_____		_____	
		_____	
_____		_____	
_____	___	_____	___
_____		_____	
		_____	
_____		_____	
_____	___	_____	___
_____		_____	
		_____	
_____		_____	
_____	___	_____	___
_____		_____	
_____		_____	

DECISION TIME

GAME TIME

Now is the time for you to move into action. You have thought about your mission and when you want to complete it. Fill in your mission and completion date below. Have your mission worded in such a way that it is clearly defined and realistic, yet challenging. To complete your mission, fill in your objectives and expected completion date. Follow and track your progress by filling in the completion date. Once you have all your objectives met, put in the date under mission. List as many objectives as you need to complete the mission. Don't forget to put in your reward under post-game report. Upon completion you are entitled to that reward, but not before. The reward should be of high value where you will work your hardest for success knowing it's the only way to relish the reward.

Mission:

_____

_____

_____

_____

_____

_____

_____

Completion Date: _____

Objectives	Expected Completion Date	Completion Date
_____	_____	_____
_____	_____	_____
_____	_____	_____
_____	_____	_____
_____	_____	_____
_____	_____	_____
_____	_____	_____
_____	_____	_____
_____	_____	_____
_____	_____	_____
_____	_____	_____

Post-Game Report

You have accomplished your mission, and you are now entitled to your reward. You have worked hard to make this happen. Enjoy the reward, and this is only one of many milestones for you. You have built your confidence so you are ready for another mission, maybe even a tougher one, maybe one more challenging and involved. Make a note on lessons learned that can benefit you in the next mission. I would encourage you to make notes as you are reaching your mission. Keep lessons learned an active part of your journal, and note them as they happen versus thinking you will remember and noting them later. In most cases, you will forget later in time what you wanted to note. In every mission, you have lessons learned that may be of a positive or negative substance. You can learn from both and better equip yourself for fewer derailments in future missions. Take time to reflect on your success. It is only one of many that you will be able to enjoy if you continue to possess the drive, confidence, and motivation.

Mission Accomplishment Date: _____

Reward:

_____

_____

_____

_____

_____

Lessons Learned:

_____

_____

_____

_____

_____

Keep a journal of your feelings and emotions while you are fulfilling your dreams and goals. Use exhibits 2 and 3 to track this. By using the exhibits, you can realize why you might not be aggressively pursuing your dreams one day and the next you are. Knowing where your emotions and feelings are will help you to readjust your life accordingly. This is important for you to realize that your feelings and emotions do affect your overall plan of success. Understanding how they interact will help you achieve your goals and dreams in a more efficient manner. The exhibits will also help you to see where your weaknesses and strengths fall. You can look at it as a self-reflection exercise.

Journal Worksheet

FEELINGS _____
_____

EMOTIONS _____
_____

WHAT DO YOU
WANT TO CHANGE _____
WITHIN YOUR CONTROL? _____

DREAMS _____
_____

HOPES/DESIRES _____
_____

FEARS _____
_____

MAJOR LIFE EVENTS _____
EXPERIENCED RECENTLY _____

WHERE IS YOUR _____
SELF-ESTEEM? _____

WHEN ARE YOU
GOING TO _____
CHANGE THINGS? _____

IS MEDICATION _____
HELPING
IF APPLICABLE? _____

WHAT DO YOU
REALIZE IS BEYOND _____
YOUR CONTROL
TO CHANGE? _____

WHAT IS YOUR _____
SUPPORT NETWORK? _____

DATE: _____
TIME: _____

ADDITIONAL NOTES:

_____
_____
_____
_____
_____
_____
_____
_____
_____
_____
_____
_____
_____
_____
_____
_____
_____
_____
_____
_____
_____
_____
_____
_____
_____
_____
_____
_____
_____
_____
_____
_____
_____
_____
_____
_____
_____
_____

EXHIBIT 2

Exhibit 3: Track your progress over time

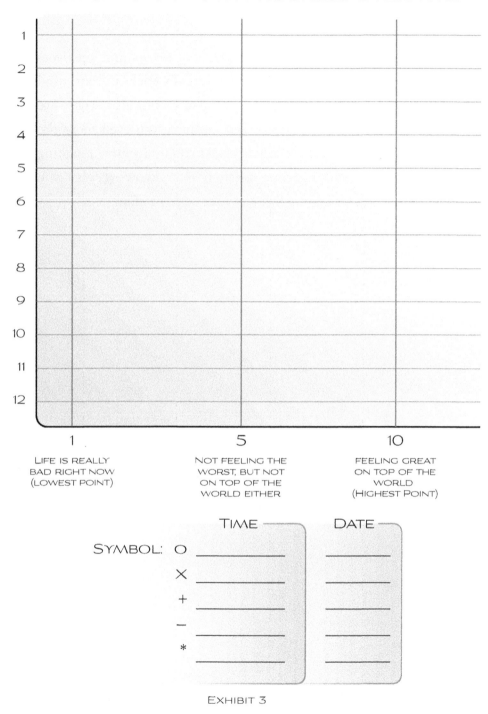

What stumbling blocks did you run across and get over? What got you to the finish line? What really sticks in your mind that makes you know you can do it the next time also? These are the kind of things to inspire and motivate you even more the next time around. What sacrifices did you find yourself making to be successful with your mission? Now knowing what you know and are capable of, what is your next mission?

THIRTEEN

TIPS TO A POSITIVE ATTITUDE

Think happy. You can be in control at any time under any situation if you remain focused. In this chapter, you will find tips to having a positive attitude. For some of you, the positive attitude is already there. For others, it takes being committed to the task to get to that point where it is automatic. You may also find tips that put a smile on your face. If you smile on the outside, you most likely will be experiencing the same on the inside. If you feel good on the inside about things going on in your life, you will project that to others on the outside.

Try it. Say something to other people that puts smiles on their faces. I do this every single day. Sometimes a person will say back, "Thank you, I needed that" or "I needed a lift today. It has been a tough day." We all should smile daily many times over. Sometimes we need someone to create that smile to realize life is not so bad. It could be worse. It is my goal to put a smile on someone's face every single day and do something nice for a person every single day, such as opening a restaurant door for someone.

The sun is powerful in so many ways. We love seeing the sun, and the value placed on the sun is different for each of you. The sun can be a powerful source for relaxation and brightness in life. The sun can represent the goodness that surrounds you and brings energy to your body and mind. Your dreams and goals can be energized by the relaxation of the sun on you. The sun can bring many things to life and bring each of us to an increased fullness and enrichment. I encourage you to experience and take in the power of the sun. Use it to give yourself a positive attitude. It is no secret to any of us the effect of little sun in the winter. The absence of the sun is more profound on some than on others. Most of us cannot wait until spring and summer arrive. The sun reenergizes us, and we come alive in many ways. On a nice, sunny summer day, many people are gathered around the lakes or paths. Have you noticed their disposition and outlook at that moment? You can see the enjoyment and warmth the sun provides. With smiles on their faces, all of them are thinking the same thing: It is such a beautiful day out and one to enjoy and cherish. It is no secret why our productivity and success can increase with the presence of the sun. Use the sun to your benefit. Find places where you can go and think using the sun's power and brightness to increase your success. Do not underestimate the value of the sun.

Living in the moment and having daily living exercises will help you do that. Don't get lost in time and think about tomorrow or yesterday. You want to do things that keep you in the moment. Enjoy what is happening now.

You do have days where things just seem to go wrong. Some are within your control, and some are not. Life is unpredictable to some extent, and when the tough times come, you will want to respond the best you can. You just don't always know when something will happen, positive or negative. The daily living exercises you incorporate in your life will be a benefit in every situation you encounter. If it is a negative situation, your exercises will help lessen the pain. Also faith and God are the first resource for us every day of our lives. These exercises not only are secondary to that resource but also have meaning and value to incorporate in your daily living.

Developing a positive outlook on things that happen daily in your life is fun. It is not difficult to make progress in this area. This pattern of exhibiting positive daily exercise will increase your overall drive to accomplish great things in your life. Daily exercises are different for everyone, and you need to find out which give you the greatest return in terms of happiness.

This can be an exciting time as well. Step out and experience different activities and thoughts. See if you have found yourself a daily exercise that energizes your passion for more of the same positive attitude. Do not fear the unknown, but know that the outcome could be positive. If not, what have you really lost? Yet the gain could be everlasting and so powerful.

DAILY LIVING EXERCISES

1. Be thankful for what you have.

2. Live to the fullest as though it is your last day.

3. Do something that makes another person smile, e.g., open the door at a shopping mall for a person.

4. Be conscious of your surroundings and environment.

5. Do something that shows you care, e.g., visit someone in the hospital, tell someone you care or love them.

6. Use financial discretion, spending only what you have.

7. Pray in the morning and before bedtime and other times as desired or needed.

8. Volunteer your time to a worthwhile charity or group organization.

9. Work on your dreams and goals.

10. Humor yourself and others.

11. Look at everything positive that happened throughout the day.

12. Give someone a smile.

13. Have alone time where you can do some thinking.

14. Find the place where you can have maximum creative thinking.

15. Reach out to someone, and say you care.

16. Listen to inspirational tapes while driving in the car.

17. Meet or talk with someone who has a positive attitude.

18. Do something out of character. Escape your comfort zone.

19. Practice speed reading.

20. Imagine positive future outcomes.

21. Stay in communication with friends and parents who will always care and be there.

22. If the past is still with you, resolve the issue and let it go. Don't let it mess up the present. Take small steps if needed.

23. Your life is yours: unique and special. Only you can travel the journey. Think about what you want your journey in life to be about.

24. Share exciting news with others.

25. Take a deep breath. It calms the mind.

26. Dispose anything and everything that is not positive in your life. Free your mind up for different thoughts that will increase your positive thinking.

27. Your happiness belongs to you, and you are in charge. Keep track of what brings you happiness.

28. Look at any mishap in a day, and ask yourself, "In five or ten years, will this matter?"

29. Clear your conscience. Tell someone who has hurt you in the past that all is forgiven.

30. Don't think about what others think of you. Just do the right thing.

31. Believe in yourself. No one else can do it for you.

32. Read something inspirational and motivational.

33. Read something humorous.

34. Post a positive quote or your goals on your refrigerator to bring humor and remind yourself where you are going in your life.

List below the things you have found to bring you positive thinking.

1. _____

2. _____

3. _____

4. _____

5. _____

6. _____

7. _____

8. _____

9. _____

10. _____

Keep focused and make it happen. Always remember there is something positive happening in your life every single day. Look for the positive, and learn from the negative. Energize yourself and look at today as another opportunity to move forward living this day to the fullest and seizing the moment.

Remember always that your life is yours to live and you are the only one who can make the most of it. Don't count on anyone else to fill your life with happiness; rather, know you have the power to control your own life.

Don't wait until tomorrow because it just never comes. Start right now and chart your plan of success. Start with doing a positive attitude exercise. Take charge. This is your life where your decisions have a huge impact on how fulfilling your life is.

FOURTEEN

LIVING LIFE
CHAIN OF HAPPINESS
& FULFILLMENT

It will be important for you to implement the living life chain of happiness and fulfillment. Remember, it is by design and plan that you are successful, not by chance and luck. By living this chain of happiness, you are moving toward your goals and dreams, planning your success. If you live for happiness and fulfillment, your likelihood of success substantially increases.

Take charge at the start of each day. The minute you wake up, take charge of the day. Have the attitude that this will be another great and productive day for you. You are in control.

Live the day. Enjoy every moment of the day. You are a work in progress, and live to make progress on your goals and dreams. Be thankful to be living today. This day is different. It is a new day.

Follow through. Continually look at what you are accomplishing throughout the day. Are you still making progress on your objectives and living the day to the fullest?

Reward yourself. You should have some rewards for all of the good work completed for the day or after a hard week. Decide how and when to reward yourself.

Monitor progress for not only the day but also the future, and work on that by doing the following:

A. Conditioning your mind

What have you noticed that would indicate your mind is being conditioned?

_____

_____

_____

_____

_____

_____

_____

Example: I am getting up earlier than I used to.

B. Performing positive self-talk exercises

List the self-talk statement(s) of the day.

_____

_____

_____

_____

_____

_____

Example: I am one day closer to realizing my dreams.

C. Being thankful at the close of the day

List all of the good things that have happened to you today.

_____

_____

_____

_____

_____

_____

Example: I received a pay raise at work.

WHAT DOES SUCCESS SPELL?

How many times have you seen words that create a larger, longer-lasting impression where the letters themselves within the word have a meaning? A word can be so powerful, but you can add more meaning by creating words within it. These words incorporate a greater sense of what the word is signifying.

I challenge you to memorize these words that stand for each letter of the word *success*. I firmly believe your motivation and inspiration will increase through this process. You might even think of your own words within the word that carry even greater significance for you.

Strategy	What's your plan to complete your dreams?
Unique	You are one of a kind and special.
Continuation	You will always be on the road toward completion.
Confidence	You are capable of reaching your dream.
Evolving	You are learning every day more about who you are.
Steps	One step at a time will build into larger steps.
Surprise	Look at what you can do. Keep up the good work.

Continue this pattern every day. See the change in what you can do. It is not *if* you can do it, but rather *when* you will do it. As time continues, notice the change in how you approach each day. Remember what success stands for, and journal your achievements. You then will have something to reflect on why you think you have made no progress. Oftentimes, we forget what we have accomplished, and by writing it down you are reminded of those achievements.

FIFTEEN

DO YOU NEED A PERSONAL LIFE COACH?

Over the years, I have been involved with counseling and coaching those in need. My objective in coaching is always to steer the person toward a positive outcome to avoid counseling. Generally speaking, coaching takes a shorter amount of time to resolve the issue, where counseling tends to involve significant issues and a larger amount of time. Through my life, I have engaged in coaching as a result of how I look at life. I have been positive and always looking for brightness even on a dark day. I have been able to inspire and motivate others to do better. I have been able to instill within individuals hope for a better tomorrow. Negative events in your life can be expected; otherwise, your life would be one hundred percent joyful and wonderful, but we know that's impossible. Therefore, the negative events simply need to be looked at in a positive light. What have I learned to avoid this happening again? What valuable lesson can be taken from this? There is no magic in coaching or counseling but rather providing you the skills and knowledge so that you can make the changes. I constantly have people telling me, "How can you always be smiling?" or "How can you enjoy life so much and be so happy?" It's how you look at life. Do you want to be part of life with having a say? Or are you having life dictate your behavior without your taking control? I have coached and counseled individuals dealing with different aspects of their lives.

How are you feeling today in your quest for happiness and life fulfillment? Answer the questions below, and see where you might be falling behind in your pursuit of life fulfillment. Give the question a 1 for almost always, 2 for most of the time, 3 for sometimes, or 4 for never.

_____ **Do you feel that you have clearly defined goals and objectives?**

_____ **Do you know what really makes you happy?**

_____ **Do you feel you have a clear vision of what your life is meant to be like?**

_____ **Do you feel every day you reach your expectations?**

_____ **Do you feel your work is indicative of what your values are?**

_____ **Do you feel your work enables you to make a contribution to others in a positive fashion?**

_____ **Is your income at the level you wish it to be?**

_____ **Are your relationships within your work environment positive?**

_____ Do you feel confined to how creative you can be at work?

_____ Are your policies and procedures enabling you to have a creative mind?

_____ Do you enjoy going to your workplace every day?

_____ Is your job position indicative of who you are in terms of personality and character?

_____ Do you find spiritual meaning in your life every day?

_____ Do you wake up every morning refreshed spiritually and wanting to live the day to the fullest?

_____ Do you feel you are following God and living according to His plan?

_____ Do you feel fully satisfied with your quality of life with regards to your personal and professional relationships?

_____ Do you feel your work and personal lives are in line with what your spiritual values and beliefs are?

_____ Do you feel good about who you are at this point in your life?

_____ Are you comfortable with experiencing your defined success?

_____ Do you realize your fears associated with success and what your obstacles are to reaching that point?

_____ **Do you move forward with your defined steps to reach your goals?**

_____ **Are you at peace when you receive love and support from others?**

_____ **Are you able to interact with others positively to get over any obstacles that remain in front of you?**

Place your score here by adding up the numbers. _____

Here is what the scores represent:

84 You are doing what it takes to reach your maximum potential in all aspects of your life. Continue doing what is working for you.

55–83 You are finding parts of your life enjoyable, but there are other aspects of your life you can improve upon to bring your whole life in total harmony.

0–54 You would find it beneficial to receive assistance from a personal life coach. You want to move forward and bring your life forward in many ways to experience and feel satisfaction, happiness, success, and a purpose to your life.

Below are areas of your life with suggestions to increase your daily dose of healthy living. These are the ones that have been the most frequently seen but do not cover every single situation.

In general, with anyone who needs a personal life coach, I always start off with positively focused questions. Let's say the issue is depression. A good question would be, "So you were depressed at some point in the past?" Let's say that you feel anger is an issue for you and expressed too often for your comfort level. You desire to lower the frequency of this happening. A good question here would be, "So you get angry sometimes?"

I always ask the person a question like, "Your perception is that..." This is meant to see what that person believes is the issue. Sometimes the perception is not always reality. Check that out for yourself, and see if this is the case with what your issue might be. Also use your senses to get responses. For instance, to feel is a sense and the question can be, "How would that feel?" To see is also another sense, and the question can be, "What do you see happening?" Also change how you look at things by using the word *will* instead of *would* or *should*. *Will* is a word that directs and motivates you to complete your objective.

Here are some other useful skills you can develop over time:

1. Develop a yes set, meaning all statements and questions have a yes answer to implement movement of your desired outcome.

2. Use questions that involve the *suppose* word. This will build and inspire creativity to solve your problem.

3. Continue to provide yourself with nonstop details of the problem. This will help you in clarifying what the real issue is, not the perceived issue, and directing you to the proper solution.

4. Ask yourself *when* questions and stay away from *if.* You leave yourself with an easy out if you use the word *if.* This also applies to the word *how*, and avoid using the word *why.* Using the word *how* creates a solution-based model for you to use.

5. Use silence to see what you are thinking, and create an environment in which you can be thinking about solutions to your issue.

Here are some other questions to ask yourself. Make notes of your answers for self-reflection:

1. What were the good things that happened?

2. Imagine having your life how you wanted it and feeling so happy. What would that be like for you?

3. What can you do right now that will make a difference for you?

4. What have you noticed at times when you have not experienced the problem, and what is different?

5. When was the last time you didn't have the problem, and what was it like?

6. Who will be the first person to notice that the problem is solved? How do you think that person will find out?

7. If your plan for success was right on schedule, what would you be doing today?

8. What would have to happen for you to reach your objective?

9. What can be different for you if you really think about it?

10. What have you done in the past that has worked?

Below are some questions I ask in my follow-up sessions that you can ask yourself:

1. What's been better for you since we last met?

2. What or who has made it easier for you to change?

3. What will it take for you to stay on this path for success?

4. What needs to happen for you to feel like you're making progress regardless of whether it's in small steps or large steps?

5. How do you resolve this predicament?

6. How is that different from the way you might have attempted to resolve this previously?

7. What is your next step on this?

8. What are your ideas to create success in the end?

9. What kind of changes have you made to make a difference in your life today?

Put yourself in a hypothetical frame of mind, and think about this. If a miracle happened to you overnight and you woke up tomorrow refreshed with a new and different life and the problem was gone, what would you be doing right now? Look at where you want to be, and think for a moment how that would feel. Put yourself in that place, and feel the satisfaction of being in that happy place. Imagine and feel the happiness and fullness of life. This will only increase your drive, motivation, inspiration, and desire to make sure you reach that place.

When an individual comes to see me, one of the first things I want to ascertain is what that person is saying in self-talk. This is important to know because this is the foundation of rebuilding the thinking process. Whatever the conflict is that you are dealing with, be aware and log what you are telling yourself. You will be amazed at the things you tell yourself that you believe are true but in reality are not. These are known as misbeliefs. When you consciously become aware of your thoughts, you will be able to decipher the truths from the misbeliefs. Remember, you feel the way you think. Try to think of something that happened to you negatively. You probably felt down or your day was ruined. Chances are that event probably wasn't a huge deal but you talked your way into feeling it. You then feel lousy, and the day just isn't the same. You also think the way you believe. This can be shown if you examine what your attitudes and feelings are. Think about your beliefs, which consist of your attitudes, feelings, reactions, behavior, and thoughts.

What are you thinking at this moment right now?

Believe it or not, you are thinking something now. You may not be able to grab it immediately, and just take a minute to retrieve it. We are always thinking something though we may not be fully aware of it.

You are on your way to making tomorrow a better day. You are on your way to making a change by thinking about what is going on in your head. Take your time to do this so that you can see the benefit.

You want to focus on the present, on the now, fixing what is happening at this very moment. Focus on your negative thoughts, and you can tell yourself that they were simply distortions. In time, you will experience a new worldview and it will be the greatest gift you will see. If you eliminate your bad thoughts, you will also substantially decrease your bad feelings. You do not need to search for your past hurts, but work on preventing negative thoughts from entering your mind. You learn how to cope. The way you think has an incredible influence on the symptoms you experience. Have you noticed how you get anxious and then you get the emotions? Your knowing how this works is another alternative to your needing a personal coach or counselor. There are people who are very well off financially, yet they worry about being broke. Why is that? These people compare themselves to others such as million-dollar hedge-fund managers. If these people understand it is not about the money but rather lifestyle and family, their thoughts change. Do you have a fear of going over bridges or through tunnels? Why is that? Rather than deal with the past, deal with the present of fixing the problem. Have you tried breathing relaxation exercises and confronting that fear? The solution is not necessarily drugs but rather looking at the fear and fixing it by the way you think. Distorted thoughts cause your emotions to go south.

SELF-ESTEEM

There are people who have problems with self-esteem. For most of the people whom I see, this is not a long-term issue. This can be short term if you are willing to really work on this.

If you blame, you are headed down a path of psychological ruin, but if you want success, then your real power begins with responsibility. Have you noticed how easily it is to blame? The real power to building your own self-esteem is to fill yourself with empowerment. You have the power to build your self-esteem or tear it down. It takes a real plan to build it versus no plan and see it fall.

I have listed below some ideas for you. The more you are able to do can only increase your chances of this being a short-term situation.

1. Daily log of emotions. List your emotions as you feel them. Keeping an accurate log with the maximum benefit requires doing it at the same time you are feeling those emotions. It is recommended to do it at the time to really know your true emotions. This will help you in seeing how you really feel.

2. Monitor self-talk. Always be aware of what you are saying. If you are aware of negative thoughts, you can turn them into positive thoughts.

3. Daily log of positive things. Keep a log of the positive things that have happened to you within a day's time. There is something positive that happens every day to every one of us. Be on the lookout for positive things. As you become more aware of how positive your life is, log the things that are making a difference for you. Your own awareness will increase the success you have in your life.

4. Completion of goals and tasks. By completing your goals and tasks, your self-esteem will increase. These goals and tasks do not need to be completed in a day or a week. List various goals and tasks that can be completed in days, weeks, and months. Your self-esteem will increase as you become more confident in your ability to finish the job.

5. Develop a promise statement to yourself similar to a mission statement. The promise statement may be something like, "I promise to increase my self-esteem and work at it each and every day. As I grow in my confidence then will I be rewarded. I will not give up or give in to what I know I really want and what I know I can truly achieve and conquer." Put this promise statement in a place where you see it continuously. Let this be a strong message to you that you have something to work for and achieve. By seeing this statement over and over, it will always be there for you to reflect on.

6. Do things that make you feel good, such as exercise. This will increase your overall attitude and affect your self-esteem. If you feel good, you are more likely to have success.

7. Associate with individuals and groups that promote self-esteem. This will be a significant help in your self-esteem growing and being nurtured. It is a fact that if we are around people who we would like to be like, we are more likely to change. It is a human reaction for us to change and adjust to who we want to be like if we are around the desired people.

8. Always remind yourself of where you want to go and who you want to be. The more you think about this, the more you want to change. If your thoughts are of a positive nature, then you will also see your actions getting you closer to your dreams and goals. Take notice that the more positive you are, the more you accomplish each day.

9. Perform a self-examination to come up with a checklist of changes you desire. Continue brainstorming and think long and hard about changes you want to make to increase your self-esteem. This may change at times depending on your progress. This self-examination centers around the core of who you are.

10. Believe in change and know that change can happen. Change will not happen unless you have the faith. Continue to believe in yourself and have the faith that it will occur.

FAMILY, FRIENDS, & RELATIONSHIPS

I have coached individuals who have conflict or tension going on within family, friends, or relationships. All of these relationships are valuable and needed in your life. Resolve differences in your relationships so that you can enjoy and value the time with that person. Life is too short, and you never want to regret not making things right. Remove the burden that you are holding inside. Don't wait for the other person to approach you.

Once you have it taken care of, you will feel so much better. It is never too late to mend things no matter how long it has been. The burden will remain until you decide to remove it. The peace you feel afterward will well be worth the time and effort, although it may be difficult to do. It is far better to get your relationships on track now. You do not want the time to come when you really need them and cannot turn to them for support. Time is valuable, so think about what you need to do.

FINANCIAL

I have assisted people with their finances to get them on track. There are things you can do to get where you feel comfortable with what you have.

First, see what your average monthly debt is by listing the following items and dollar amounts for each: auto loans, school loans, personal loans, time-payment loans, and credit cards. No need to list your mortgage or rent at this time. Your debt rate is the percentage of your take-home pay that goes to pay your debts. Most have a debt rate of around twelve percent. To find this, enter your total monthly debt and divide that amount by your monthly take-home pay. The result will be your debt rate. This is one indicator of where you stand in relation to debt. If you find you do have a debt problem, do not worry because you can decrease your debt percentage.

Knowing you have a debt problem and acknowledging this is the first step in resolving this situation. It would be advisable for you to cut up all of your credit cards. Cut expenses to only absorbing those that are absolutely necessary. Cut your expenses by ten percent on your grocery bills, utility bills, and auto expenses. Then shift this savings to reduce your monthly debt payments. Earn extra cash by seeking a part-time job, or try to get overtime at your full-time job. You can sell any valuables and apply that money to your debt. These are only a few of the things you can commit yourself to doing.

Make a list of all your other expenses. This list would include the following: groceries, dining out, household, heat, electricity, telephone, clothing, doctor, dentist, prescriptions, barber, beauty, recreation, gifts, auto repairs, auto gas, insurance, education, savings, fees, and miscellaneous. Add these amounts up, and for each category, reduce your spending by a certain amount. Do not cut rent, mortgage, auto loans, credit cards, personal loans, taxes, or other loan expenses, which you should be increasing your payments for.

Here are some things to plan and commit to:

1. You want to pay off your lowest credit card balance first. Put it on your calendar when that payoff will happen. This way you will be more committed if you have it down on paper.

2. Are you looking for ways to get some new cash coming in? What about a yard sale or selling your services such as babysitting, pet-sitting, cleaning things, building things, or painting things?

3. Call the credit card companies, and ask them what they will settle for. Credit card companies most likely will settle for less than what is owed. Seek a family

member or anyone else you can think of to possibly loan the money to you at a lower rate.

4. When possible, get a second opinion. There are times when a second opinion will save you money.

5. When you are looking at purchasing something, ask yourself these questions: Do I really need it? Is it necessary that I have it? This can be used for the simplest things such as buying a candy bar.

6. Contact the three major credit bureaus, and obtain a copy of your credit record. The three major credit bureaus are Equifax FKA CSC Credit Services, Experian, and TransUnion. You may notice the bureau contains information that is inaccurate, false, or missing. If you notice anything at all on the bureau that you disagree with, write a letter. It is a good idea to check your credit on a regular basis to make sure it contains no surprises that require a response. A letter to the bureau explaining the discrepancy will become part of your file and attached to anyone requesting your report such as a car dealership.

It is much easier to get yourself in control when the debt issue is not totally out of control. If you sense your debt is getting out of control, deal with it immediately before it becomes worse.

Let me touch on four different areas: Job, Spiritual, Marriage, and Divorce.

JOB

I have seen people who have issues with their job. Oftentimes the job is not one they like or the people they work with are making the job not worth it any longer. If the issues are worker related, have you sat down with the individual(s) to discuss the situation? Oftentimes it is simply a matter of communication and misunderstanding. Most people can work things out if they are approached about a situation. Maybe there is a coworker who you trust and will be a mediator between the parties. If you like the job and there is a personality clash or some other conflict, it is far better to resolve the conflict and enjoy the job again. If you believe a coworker does not like you for some reason, ask that coworker at an appropriate time and in a nonthreatening manner. You may want to say something like, "I noticed you did [insert action here] the other day, and I didn't know exactly what you meant." Another example might be, "I wasn't real clear on what happened the other day. Would you help me understand?" You do not want to confront the parties in a threatening manner, which puts them on the defensive. I always would advise you to continue working that job until you find another one. You want to be able to count on that job as a reference.

SPIRITUAL

It is important that a person has a spiritual base. All people have spiritual bases, but they don't always know it. A person may find a spiritual base at a later time when it is a time of crisis and life is at a crossroads. Life is extremely challenging. How many times have you thought there must be an easier way to deal with something?

I could not live life without being a believer. God is my spiritual base and my guiding force in all things that happen whether it is in my thoughts or behaviors. I live every day believing certain things. I believe that things happen for a reason. I do not always know the reason why something happened, but it is something that at some point will be communicated to me. I do not question why things happen. Everything is planned by God, and His plan is not always laid out to me. But the fact that I believe creates the trust in Him that a plan exists. We are watched over and cared for, although it is not always evident to us.

I can remember many years ago when I was by the hospital bed with my girlfriend's mother. She was dying. Her mother wanted her last rites to be given to her. I arranged for a pastor to come and perform this for her. I was there along with her daughter and mother. Her mother was going fast, and I didn't know if the pastor would make it in time. The pastor showed up, and the mother was calmed by this act. I could tell that she was ready to go and be with the Lord. She was not one who prayed or thought often about the Lord, but when the final moments came, she wanted to be saved. She was at peace now and comforted by the Lord, and she knew she was going to the best place there was. About a half hour later, she passed away. I will never forget how she looked at us before she gave her final breath and closed her eyes. She looked at us, and she knew she was going. But she was in peace and saved. Even though she did not place her trust in God through most of her life, she knew that she had been watched over by God.

We do not need to believe for any of us to be watched over and cared for. My position as visitation minister at church is to visit individuals in the hospice, hospital, or other places who have requested a minister to come and pray for them. They are in a time of need and know that God will provide peace and comfort to their situation. These people live by the grace of God and hope for their recovery. They also are aware that recovery is not guaranteed, but they know their best hope for recovery is placing their trust in God. They believe that if it is to happen it will happen. They believe that a plan does exist for them and are accepting of the fact that death is a possibility. It is not for me to decide who chooses to believe. I know the difference and see the difference in people. Life to those who believe is one of peace, comfort, forgiveness, caring, and so much more. This is the road that I love to be on. This is where I want to be and would encourage everyone to join me, but it is up to every one of you individually.

When you have a rough day, where do you go? Who do you rely on? What do you do that brings you peace and comfort? These are certainly questions that you should ask yourself. Life gives each of us our ups and downs. It is in your best interest to search for your answers to these questions. This question of spirituality can be a tough one for some people. We all hope for the best of everything in life. This life is our only life. How do you plan to live with maximum happiness? You have a belief system that you turn to in times of darkness. The question is, do you know what yours is? And how often do you turn to it?

I always inform people I coach of where my faith lies. I have seen individuals who do not believe, and I encourage all to seek God. I have also seen these same individuals turn to God and their lives have been changed. Unfortunately, sometimes a life is cut short. This is exactly why life needs to be valued. We do not know when our time has come, and when it comes we do not know if it is sudden. How many people do you know have passed away and you wonder why it happened? How could that have happened at such a young age? There must have been something that went wrong. These are questions we all ask ourselves. Have you decided to answer your own questions?

In my work as a firefighter and EMT, I have seen things that some people will never see. I have seen fatalities, and the hardest of them all is when it happens to children and young people. I can only hope they have experienced life enough at that point. I have wanted to pray over the critical patients, but policy did not allow me to do so. I have prayed quietly for their recovery. I have been witness to many who were not revived after suffering cardiac arrest. In most cases, families were there for this event. I have prayed in private for their loss. My exposure to trauma, tragedy, and loss has filled me with desire to get everything out of life and not take for granted that I am on Earth. I have been blessed with the opportunity to be in this line of work and see how great life can be and how fast it can be taken away. How blessed do you feel today?

Marriage

I have coached individuals on marriage. Most of the time the problem revolves around communication. Communication should be the easiest thing to do, but oftentimes it's not done. Part of this is that we assume too much and believe another person knows what we are thinking or why we behave in such a manner. Unless we have dialogue, it is amazing what we do not know about each other.

When I see married couples or even one and not the other, there are certain points that I mention. These points you can use daily in your desire to have your marriage be even more complete and whole. Every one of these does not need to be done daily, but regularly fulfill some of these and keep that love alive and on fire.

1. **Accept your significant others for who they are, and don't wish they were somebody else.**

Most people believe if the other person changes, they would be happy. If you believe in love, unconditional love, then your thinking also changes. You are less demanding and more accepting of who that person is. You then become aware consciously and make the changes.

2. **Don't keep track of all that's going wrong.**

It is common nature for us to be aware of what is going wrong and less aware of what is positive and right. If you are aware of what is going right, that will override the negative thinking going on.

3. **Have fun. Enjoy life.**

Share together everything, and rejoice in the times where you laugh and smile about things. Keep life simple and exciting, and keep that sense of humor going.

4. **Unless it is significant and meaningful, no need to correct your partner.**

How many times have you been somewhere and heard one

party tell the other "No, there were only ten people at that event" or "No dear, the cost was $12, not $10." There is no need to correct your partner on this because it only creates hostility. Unless it really means something to correct the other person, you are better off to just not say anything.

5. Pick your battles.

Decide which battles you wish to confront the other one on. If you thought about it, there are numerous events each week you would love to talk about. Decide which ones are really worth going to this extreme. Make sure that you bring this battle on when the time is right. Know when your significant other is more likely to be open to discussion. Do not use your significant other as somebody you can just blow off your anger on. There are many things to get upset about, but don't take it out against your partner.

6. Take time to be with your partner.

Make sure you give your significant other the time they should receive. It's fairly easy to let other things take priority. Be conscious of who your partner is and of your responsibility within the relationship. Invite your partner with you to events, and you will see your partner respond positively. Your partner may not go, but you will get a pat on the back for putting the offer out.

7. Master communication skills.

When you talk with your significant other, don't get defensive on things and make sure you are diplomatic in your communication. It would be beneficial and wise for both of you to learn the art of communication. Your attitude is important to how these discussions go. It is beneficial for you to learn more than teach. It is beneficial for you to listen more than speak. It is beneficial for you to absorb and know what is being said more than react to your first gut feeling. Think about what is being said before reacting to it.

DIVORCE

Many individuals need coaching after a divorce, and some end up needing counseling. Divorce is not an easy thing, especially when kids are involved. Both parties should make an honest attempt to be cordial with each other. Although there is significant animosity between the parents, the kids should not have to deal with that. For the kids' sake, be respectful of each other when the kids are present. Also, do not degrade the other when you are with your kids. There are things you can do if you must to move on with your life as far as your spouse goes, but be loving and caring to your kids. These are some of the things you may wish to try in order to move on.

1. **Clean house.**

Remove everything that reminds you of your ex. If you have nothing in sight that reminds you of your ex, then your chances increase that you won't think of your ex. Also try to think of other things and not your ex. Do activities that will not remind you of your ex. It is very important for you to detach from your ex in every way you can. Avoid any temptation to contact your ex. If kids are involved, then there must be some contact, but keep it limited and focused. Cleaning house is much more difficult when kids are involved.

What are you going to do?

_____

_____

_____

2. Stay clear of your ex.

With kids involved, it would not be possible to do this. But if you have no kids involved, then work and reside in an area where you are not crossing paths with your ex. Do not frequent places where you know the ex goes. Stay away from communicating about the ex to others. Look ahead, and think about the person you want to meet.

What are you going to do?

_____

_____

3. Mediate in some fashion.

Decide which mediation will fit best for you. The subjects might be focused on the negatives of the ex or on the qualities that you want the future spouse to possess. Or maybe it is on another person altogether. Mediation is beneficial and helpful. Your thoughts need to be open to the process. If you believe it will not help prior to trying it, then you only increase your chances that it won't work. For some, it is a powerful tool to use.

You have to look at whether you believe in this and, if so, have an open mind to receive the greatest rewards possible. If you have not ever been through this process, then it is one you should try.

What are you going to do?

_____

_____

4. Be happy and smile often.

Remind yourself to smile and put the best light on the situation. Maybe you can have someone you know remind you to put that smile on. When you smile, it helps that day be a better one. Smiling is contagious. It is something we never see enough of. A smile sends a powerful nonverbal message. A smile is like the sun where it brings warmth and happiness. I am sure you have noticed others smile and wonder what that person is happy about. Turn it around, and smile, and have others wonder what you are happy about. Wouldn't this world be a better place if we always saw a smile everywhere we went? Imagine.

What are you going to do?

_____

_____

5. Be thankful for what you do have.

Add up everything you can be thankful for, and practice reminding yourself of these blessings in life. You could have less. You have the opportunities in life to have more. Every day you wake up, give thanks. Work at what you would want to have. Always remember you really cannot have everything you want, so pick which ones mean the most to you. Don't look at what others have, but at what you are willing to work hard at to get. Make your list, and see which things you will appreciate the most. Keep in mind that some people who have little are the happiest.

What are you going to do?

_____

_____

6. Join a group.

There are groups around where you live. Get involved in groups that will assist you in going forward. The city in which you live and the chamber of commerce are good places to start. In the city you live, look for events to attend and all the organizations that you can be part of. Social networking and interaction is powerful in moving on. Join groups that you can relate to and will be a benefit for you. Divorce groups, in particular, are in every city or close by and provide a valuable resource for you. Check your local church for information. You will be surprised about how many other people are in the same position as you. You are never very alone.

What are you going to do?

_____

_____

7. Exercise often.

Exercise is a great stress reliever and gives you peace. Find the exercise that you most enjoy, such as walking, dancing, swimming, and hiking. Health clubs provide a good forum for you. Being with others exercising provides inspiration and motivation. It feels good, you feel better, and life seems to be better. There are many clubs or groups to be part of at no cost to you. Check to see if any of them sound worthwhile. Remember exercise is good for not only your body but also your mind.

What are you going to do?

_____

_____

8. Keep busy and enjoy the sun.

Try to keep busy with different things. Get with friends, parents, and family, or start working on your projects and goals. Enjoy the sun, which will put a smile on your face and help you see the beauty that surrounds you. Experiencing the sun will enhance your mood, and you will feel better about the day. Your mind will be opened to the future that you desire. Keeping busy with the right choices is positive. Choose carefully what you keep busy with. Not everything you choose may be beneficial. Do not be influenced by others who do not have your best interests in mind. Your life is full of choices, but use them wisely.

What are you going to do?

_____

_____

9. Do not get involved in a relationship right away.

Stay on your own until you know you are over the last relationship. Develop your own self, and know what you desire in the next relationship. Take the time to enjoy what you do have, and whoever that person is will be there when you decide to commit to another relationship. This will be the best time to focus on you. You need this to be clear on where you are going and what you want. Don't be tempted to get involved thinking someone else has the answers for you or the solution. This oftentimes only creates increased confusion on what you need to do. Someone else doesn't know everything about your situation, and their input could add unnecessary time to finding your answers to moving on. Unless they have walked in your shoes, do they really know where you are at or what you have been through?

What are you going to do?

_____

_____

What do you think? Do you need a personal life coach? Where is your life at? Are you on track for success or looking for assistance? There is nothing wrong with having a life coach at a time when your life is out of control. Many believe that they can figure things out on their own as life passes by. Are you in this camp, or wanting to get things figured out and willing to seek assistance? This is your life, and you only get one. I would urge you to contact me if you just don't know where to go or what to do.

Your life is the now, today. Not the next day or week but now. You have an opportunity now to look at your life and where it is. Making decisions now will affect your life as it continues.

Stay focused. What do you want in life? Do you know? Is life passing you by as you remain in one place, or are you moving in life, creating opportunities along the way?

I have asked many questions, some difficult, some easy. This was in hopes that you will do some searching for answers. I also hope the answers you find missing are the drive that creates a passion to live life as you want.

SIXTEEN

WEBSITE

The website www.liveforthemoment.life is designed with you in mind. It is designed to help you in your daily life to achieve your goals and inspire you in maintaining a positive attitude and outlook in life. On the other hand if you are falling short of having that constant positive attitude then this will increase that. For those of you that are looking for positive things in your life then this is especially for you. This will assist in filling your mind with a positive attitude and a thirst for life whereby you can enjoy and thrive.

On the web site I have a "Thought of the Week" published every week. This is a phrase that I have located, and which acts as a catalyst for action by virtue of its substance. I have the thought of the week along with a short author biography, and then I go further and challenge you to do some things. The thought of the week is designed to motivate you and my action of the week for you, puts you into action. This works if you give yourself this challenge and then you follow through on the plan.

I encourage you to take advantage of this and see for yourself.

You can also choose how you want the "Thought of the Week" delivered to you. You can either go back to the web site as often as you need to and be reminded of what your action is for that week or you can send me a request and I will email it to you so you have it at your disposal at all times. I would recommend you send me the request to have it delivered to you so that you have an easy reference to the "Thought of the Week".

If you have not already purchased the book, I highly recommend you do that as well. Once you have followed the guidelines in the book and you are experiencing the positive changes that are changing your life, then let me know. My second book will consist of testimonies from others on how this book has changed their life. I need your feedback for consideration. Another variable that can influence change is change that others have made and their testimony. This can be a strong motivational for others to accomplish their goals and dreams knowing that others did it despite the obstacles and barriers.

Just remember, you have the power and control to reach your destiny. It is within your means to reach your dreams and goals. Don't wait for tomorrow. Start today by going to "Thought of the Week" at www.liveforthemoment.life and order the book.

SEVENTEEN

ESTATE PLANNING

Do you want to avoid probate?

Do you want to protect your assets?

Do you want to control your assets?

Do you want to be assured your estate will be distributed as you desire after you pass on?

You probably have thought of these questions in the past, and they are very important in your process of estate planning. In this chapter, I will articulate why these questions are important and what is available for you to be fully prepared.

None of us knows when our lives will end, but we certainly want to enjoy our lives while we can. Likewise, when we are enjoying our lives we also want to be prepared if the unthinkable happens. Death is unexpected, or it is expected when the quality of life decreases over time. In either case, you may not be in a right or competent state of mind to prepare your necessary documents.

Discussing what happens to your estate is not an enjoyable or pleasant discussion, and many try to avoid it or wait until it's too late. But there is also peace and comfort in knowing that your estate planning is taken care of. Therefore, the time to do your estate planning is now, if you are competent to do so.

Estate planning is commenced not only for personal reasons but also with the beneficiaries in focus. Most parents want the transition of their estate to go smoothly and without problems. They do not want their children to relive their parents' deaths over and over. Likewise, the children or beneficiaries are relieved to know it's been taken care of. Some people have had to liquidate estates where no estate plan existed.

I knew four children whose mother had passed away, and their father had passed away years earlier. Their mother had no living trust. Wills existed, but they were contested in probate court. Wills, unlike living trusts, have to go through probate court to finalize the estate. A will does not give anyone the power to transfer assets, so court intervention is necessary to have assets moved to another individual. A living trust does give authority to others so that court intervention can be avoided. The daughter told me they had $40,000 in attorney fees. This situation broke the family apart. It was very traumatic and expensive, and their mother's death had to be relived time and time again through probate. Probate court is not the place you want to be.

In the seminars that I conduct on estate planning, I am always surprised at what I learn from the attendees. At least half of the people in attendance believe that a will will avoid probate. However, a will is not sufficient.

There are three reasons why people don't do estate planning. The first one is DENIAL. Nothing will ever happen to me, but to someone else. We know that's false. Every day the media mentions people killed in motor vehicle accidents. Were those people prepared in the event that they suddenly died? I am safe from ever being in harm's way. We choose not to think about what could happen, and by doing so we don't do anything. We hear and read about death occurring at all ages and believe that we will be lucky enough to avoid anything traumatic happening to any of us.

The second reason people don't do estate planning is PROCRASTINATION. You will get to it but not now—maybe in the near future. However, you never get to it and the unthinkable happens—then it's too late. Do not put off what you can do today. Do not bet your life will continue until whenever that time in the future comes. For some of you, tomorrow will never come. Today has arrived, but tomorrow is always coming and a day later.

The third reason is LACK OF KNOWLEDGE. Once you have this information, the decision can be made. The decision is an easy one once you have the information.

Estate planning involves the creation of a living trust. A living trust is not only a legal document if called into court but also a private document. Unless the living trust is contested, it remains a private document and stays a family matter. The living trust allows you to control the management of your property. You can also change the living trust at any point. This is called the revocable living trust, and you have this option whether you are married or single. A living trust also provides for the distribution of your property upon your death. Once the death certificate is received by the successor trustee, distribution of the property can begin. The living trust remains alive for twenty-one years after the last creator passes on. This is beneficial in many ways. For instance, a son may leave his share of the estate in the living trust so that creditors cannot attach claim to that money. He can keep the living trust active for twenty-one years if he wishes. Therefore, creditors do not have access to the money.

The living trust is created by a person called either a settler, creator, or trustee. All of the terms mean the same thing. If a husband and a wife create a revocable living trust, they are known as the settlers, creators, or trustees. At any point they can change the living trust. Within the living trust, they have named a successor trustee. This person is responsible for liquidating the estate when both trustees have passed on, but not until then. If the husband and wife have five children, then the successor trustee has the responsibility of making sure the children receive estate proceeds if so ordered in the living trust. The twenty-one years survival of the living trust starts when the last spouse passes on or both of them expire together.

In essence, the creator(s) have given the power of the pen to another person. The power of the pen enables the successor trustee to transfer property without court intervention. This concept provides for the smooth transition of all property.

The living trust is created because it avoids probate. This is also important to remember because this is the only tool that provides for no court intervention. Most people want to avoid probate for various reasons: attorney costs, probate fees, time consumption, and the reliving of the death(s).

The living trust is simple to create and far less expensive than probate. You retain control of your property, and you know what will happen to your property. The living trust can also save death taxes and provide lawsuit and divorce protection.

Components of a living trust are as follows:

Trust Agreement. This contains the names of the trustee(s), successor trustee(s), beneficiaries, and how the estate is to be divided up. It also contains clauses, e.g., missing person, spend-thrift, contestability, and other important verbiage such as HIPPA. The trust agreement is the heart of the living trust. This is explicit in what will happen to the estate. If a beneficiary has a drug problem, for example, then the creator has the power to state that only a certain amount of money each month goes to the beneficiary rather than the full amount. It could be monthly, weekly, or any other time specified. The point is that the living trust agreement can be created in any way—there are no boundaries to what you can do.

Pour-Over Wills. This transfers at death any assets outside of the trust into the trust. These assets could be, for example, dishes, furniture, and paintings.

Certificate of Trust. This certificate is used to assure simple asset transfers or funding. This certificate proves that a living trust exists.

Health Care Directive. This document, also known as a living will, authorizes termination of life support systems if there is a terminal illness.

Health Care Power of Attorney. This document is now included in the health care directive. It authorizes the person you name to make any and all health care decisions for you if you are unable to do so on your own.

Durable Power of Attorney. This document authorizes a person you name to manage your property if you become incapacitated.

Successor Trustee Instructions. This is used after the last trustee passes on. It contains instructions for the successor trustee on how to liquidate the estate.

Trust Transfer Documents. These documents are used when transferring assets into your trust.

Do you have these documents prepared and ready in case something happens to you? If not, you still have an opportunity to get this accomplished. Now is the time to contact me and make it happen so that you have peace of mind.

Let's talk about a funeral expense trust policy. This is a popular tool in protecting some of your assets from Medicaid. A living trust is designed to avoid probate. This funeral expense policy is designed to make sure you have money set aside for final expenses that cannot be taken by Medicaid. Most people interested in estate planning end up creating a living trust. A funeral expense trust policy is not as important as a living trust. If a person does not have the financial means to pay for final expenses, family or others will have to pay the bill. A funeral expense trust policy is an aspect of estate planning but is secondary to a living trust. The living trust is the overall tool to avoid probate and is of utmost importance to create. If you end up in a nursing home, for instance, you will be forced to spend down your assets to an acceptable level determined by Medicaid. You will be left basically broke.

The maximum allowed for a funeral expense trust is $15,000. Not too long ago it was $12,500.

The benefits for a funeral expense trust are as follows:

1. Funds are protected from Medicaid spend–down.

2. The trust is the policy owner and beneficiary.

3. The trust will pay funeral costs with any excess going to the estate of the insured.

4. There is no cost to you.

5. There are no trust fees.

6. It can be used in addition to any other trust you may already have.

7. The process is simple and fast.

8. You can fund a funeral policy with money from another policy known as the 1035 Exchange.

The 1035 Exchange is a way to transfer money directly from one insurance policy to another without creating tax consequences for the policy owner. If you have a paid-up policy for under $15,000, then you could do a 1035 Exchange. Medicaid can force you to spend down your life insurance policies, and this is a tool to exempt $15,000 from being attached. Life insurance policies generally are meant to go to beneficiaries. The 1035 Exchange will assure that the beneficiaries will receive any proceeds left over from the funeral burial expenses.

The average funeral cost is $8,495, according to the U.S. Federal Trade Commission.

It is not easy for beneficiaries to come up with this money.

The funeral trust policy takes care of this problem for family members.

The policy is free of market risk, the principal is guaranteed, the proceeds avoid probate costs and federal income tax, and some plans have a defined growth rate.

It is no secret why these trusts are popular.

The chance of your ending up in a nursing home is more likely than not. The time to plan for this in NOW. You have the ability to exclude your policy as an asset in order to qualify for Medicaid and supplemental security income. Funds used for funeral expenses are protected from creditors, such as nursing homes, hospitals, and lawyers.

Asset Strategies Group, of which I am president, offers seminars on these topics frequently across the Twin Cities, Minnesota, area. Asset Strategies Group offers substantial services to clients. We always say we are very special because we go far and above in what we offer and believe there is no comparison between us and others. When you purchase a living trust, you will receive the following services at one price—in effect, you are receiving service forever at one price:

Answers to all of your questions. No matter how lengthy or involved the questions are, we will answer them all.

Convenience. We will come to where you are. You will not have to travel or go anyplace. The business will be done in the comfort of your premises and where you have the information readily accessible.

Funded living trust. We want to know you have a working living trust and, therefore, will fully complete this process. This process involves making sure your assets are placed in the living trust. We want to make sure your living trust is completely funded.

Settled estate. Although the living trust has instructions outlining how to settle the estate, we do not hesitate to say, "Call us" to your successor trustee. Your successor trustee can call our office to ask for our assistance. We will help your successor trustee through your estate distribution.

Reviewed living trust. We will review your living trust every twelve to eighteen months. This is done to ensure that your living trust is in working order. Often a living trust is set aside and forgotten about until we review it and notice that not all of the assets are in the living trust. All assets need to be named in the living trust. For example, a vehicle may be purchased after the living trust was created. Upon review of your trust, we will notice that and have it corrected.

Value. The value of our product and the customer service given far outweigh the cost. The customer service we provide is the best there is. A percentage of new business comes from referrals. We know that if clients are extremely happy and satisfied, they will tell everyone about us.

Referral program. If you refer a client to us, we will apply a discount to the product they are purchasing and we will also mail you a check for appreciation of the referral.

A living trust is the document you want to look into. This chapter covers the basics of a living trust. It explains what a living trust is and what it accomplishes, but there is much more involved in a living trust than just what's contained in this chapter.

ABOUT THE
AUTHOR

Craig Gordon grew up in Brooklyn Center, Minnesota outside of Minneapolis, Minnesota. He attended North Hennepin Community College and then attended Metropolitan State University earning majors in psychology and business. His parents reside in Maple Grove, Minnesota as does his one sister.

Craig has been a resident of Fridley, Minnesota for 23 years. He has been active in the community in different ways; Mayor of Fridley candidate, Fridley Charter Commission member 10 years, Fridley Firefighter 21 years, State Senator candidate, State Representative candidate, Fridley Lions member 14 years, Fridley 49ers Committee member 4 years, Empty Bowls Committee chair 8 years. Craig has started and sold companies in the past; video arcade, singles dating company, collection agency, and roller derby league (second one in the State of Minnesota). He presently does counseling and coaching which has been going for 14 years and previously a lay chaplain. Craig is passionate about helping others get in touch with themselves about living for the moment.

For the last 14 years Craig has touched many people in realizing their true potential to reach their destiny. Life can be cut short for any of us and not knowing when that time is should be a signal for us that every moment is worth living. Set yourself free, enjoy life, treasure the moment, know your potential, and bring your dreams and goals to life. Craig also will do motivational speaking for any size group upon request.

To request an appearance by Craig Gordon please contact Craig Gordon at **csg488@qwestoffice.net** or at the office 763-571-8285. You can also view the website at **www.liveforthemoment.life** Craig will travel anywhere in the country to speak.